The ART OF SOAP MAKING

BY MERILYN MOHR

A Harrowsmith Contemporary Primer

A Complete Introduction to the History and Craft of Fine Soapmaking

Complete recipes for hand soaps, herbal shampoos, natural toothpaste, vegetarian soap, laundry soap and many rich and fragrant homemade soaps

©Copyright 1979 by Camden House
Publishing (a division of Telemedia
Communications Inc.)

Second printing 1980   Fifth printing 1988
Third printing 1982   Sixth printing 1991
Fourth printing 1984   Seventh printing 1993

Canadian Cataloguing in Publication Data

Mohr, Merilyn
  The art of soap making

(A Harrowsmith contemporary primer)
Includes bibliographical references and index.
ISBN 0-920656-03-X

1. Soap.   I. Title.   II. Series.

TP991.M64 1979   668'.124219   C80-009013-6

Cover art by Pat Michener
Photography and illustrations by Jurgen Mohr

Printed and bound in Canada by
D.W. Friesen & Sons Ltd.
Altona, Manitoba

Printed on acid-free paper

Published by Camden House Publishing
(a division of Telemedia Communications Inc.)

Camden House Publishing
7 Queen Victoria Road
Camden East, Ontario K0K 1J0

Camden House Publishing
Box 766
Buffalo, New York 14240-0766

Trade distribution by
Firefly Books
250 Sparks Avenue
Willowdale, Ontario
Canada M2H 2S4

Box 1325
Ellicott Station
Buffalo, New York 14205

Foreword

I always feel a kind of alchemy at work when a batch of homemade soap is being made, a process that is at once deeply primitive and highly elegant. Unlike commercial soaps of today, a bar of handcrafted soap seems to have a character and richness of its own, and from the strange and streaked concoction my first landlady grated into her washtub to the herbal bar I washed with this morning, handmade soap has never failed to excite me.

Soapmaking cannot help but appeal to one's sense of frugality — one can make a year's supply of fine quality bars for pennies each — but beyond the economics, this is a folk art that makes ecological sense. Handmade soap contains nothing you do not add yourself, and the multiple additives that now find their way into both bathing and laundry soaps can happily be avoided.

My own interest in pure homemade soaps eventually led to the formation of a small country soapmaking business, which in turn led me deeper into the history and lore of soap and which, finally, helped spawn this book.

I am indebted to the many kind people who have generously given their time and special knowledge in providing research material, especially the soapmakers, both past and present, whose experiences and expertise have added much to this book. I am also greatly appreciative of the assistance provided by my editor and publisher and of the moral support lent by my family and friends.

It is my hope that this book will move others to take up an art that has been largely lost, and in the process discover the unique pleasures of handmade soap.

—*Merilyn Mohr*

for my mother

who helped me appreciate
the past with faith in
the future

Contents

1 Tallow Ho

"Soap and education are not as sudden as a massacre, but they are more deadly in the long run...."

— *Mark Twain*

One of the various interpretations of our country's name has it deriving from the Cree word *Kanâta,* meaning something which is very neat or clean. Judging from the half billion pounds of cleaning products consumed in 1977 by households within these borders, the name is well-deserved.

That soap, and our addiction to it, is a fairly recent phenomenon may come as a surprise. Not too far in the distant past, however, most people would have agreed with Mark Twain that "soap and education are not as sudden as a massacre, but they are more deadly in the long run."

It appears that soap, along with smallpox and firewater, was introduced to this continent by Europeans. In the scores of accounts of first meetings between white man and red, mention of aboriginal hygienic practices is conspicuously scarce. Ignoring specifics, most observers of the strange inhabitants of the New World simply registered repugnance at the odours and oddities of a culture they didn't understand. David Thompson, a Canadian explorer and mapmaker of the early nineteenth century, offers a singularly perceptive observation:

The natives are as neat in their persons as circumstances will allow, but without soap there is no effectual cleanliness; this we know very well who too often experience the want of it. Take soap from the boasted cleanliness of the civilized man, and he will not be as cleanly as the savage who never knew its use.

Aboriginal Indians had little need for soap. Their clothing, like that of the Eskimo, was made of animal hides which were simply brushed off or replaced when they became worn. Despite pressure from proselytizing pioneers, many local Indians refused to take up European dress because "their women cannot wash them when they be soiled . . . therefore, they had rather go naked than be lousy."

In fact, the reverse occurred, and many of the earliest settlers adopted Indian dress when their European clothes expired. The application of so-called civilized standards to native wear often met with unfortunate results. In several pioneer recollections, the story is told of a young girl who undertook to clean her one and only garment, a deerskin shift. She dipped it into a tub of lye-water, only to see it shrivel before her eyes, forcing her to take tearful refuge in her blankets.

Although they did not use soap, bathing was an integral part of early Canadian Indian life. With most encampments located near streams, rivers, and lakes, swimming was frequent. Washing, however, served more than hygienic purposes. Together with fasting and celibacy, elaborate ablutions cleansed the body and soul in preparation for communion with supernatural beings. Ritual bathing was compulsory as a prelude to hunting, healing, and initiation. Young Indian babies were bathed frequently in cold water to toughen them. Although this practice must have led to the untimely demise of some newborns, it ensured that only the fit survived to withstand the endurance test that was the native's life style of early times.

Most astonishing to European newcomers was the Indian sweat bath. Although Teutonic in origin, this steamy ritual had all but disappeared in Europe before the discovery of America. Surviving in Finland as the sauna, and common to Africa and the Pacific Islands, many believe the sweat bath to have reached its highest development in the New World.

As early as 1653, in his report to Cardinal de Lugo regarding the "barbarians" of New France, Father Bressani describes the sweat bath of the Hurons:

They use hot baths, but in a very Barbarous manner; they enclose large stones, red-hot, in a little cabin, where 15 or 20 persons come together, seated like Apes, who touch one another closely, and remain there during whole hours, — working themselves, while singing violently, into an excessive perspiration; and on issuing thence, even at the beginning of winter, they plunge into some half-frozen lake or river, from which, inexplicable though it seem, they return without distress. They do this from superstition, for cleanliness, for health, and for pleasure....

Besides being a sanitary and religious device, the sweat bath, accompanied by sudorific herbs, was a panacea for all diseases. The fumes of wild horsemint or balsam needles scattered on the coals were inhaled for colds. As a relief to sore muscles and rheumatism, witch hazel twigs were steeped in water heated by hot rocks to produce the soothing steam.

With increased exposure to traders and settlers, the aboriginal Indians gradually adopted many of the white man's habits, among them, the use of soap. In the mid 1800s, among West Coast Indians, a piece of soap of a finger's thickness was worth four marten pelts. Translated from trader terminology, this was a high price, since a blanket could be had for ten. Among the native children in mission settle-

JACK CANUCK
TAR SOAP.
JOHN TAYLOR & CO.
TORONTO, CANADA.

ments, a sliver of soap was often the coveted prize of schoolyard games.

In the biography of William Duncan, a lay preacher of extraordinary missionary fervour, soap becomes accessory to a well-intentioned scheme to convert the natives of Fort Simpson on the northwest Pacific coast. This zealous Christian persuaded the Indians to renounce their rich heritage and relocate in a European-style village. Gone were the medicine men, moccasins, potlatches and totems. Among the vows made by potential community members was the pledge to be clean. The Indians renounced their spirit-gods for the monotheism of Christianity and eagerly embraced the European way of life. Duncan encouraged his charges to plant garden plots and build frame houses. In the late 1800s, together with a forge, carpentry shop, sawmill, and brick kiln, he started a soap factory.

The common dictum that cleanliness is next to godliness implies that soap and washing have long been endorsed by the church. The fact is that Duncan was applying a relatively new principle of piety.

Traditionally, Christian dogma viewed the body as a temporary vessel for the soul. Undue concern with bodily functions was considered detrimental to the spirit. As time progressed, fundamentalist sects warned against the physical being itself as a potential source of evil. The act of dressing took on overtones of the Original Sin, fostering an overdeveloped sense of modesty. Even in private, disrobing was sinful. Bathing itself was discouraged, often deplored.

The Romans, along with Jews and Greeks, espoused a vastly different philosophy. In these cultures, the body was held in great respect, as a gift from the gods. Sanitation and body cleanliness became a major preoccupation with the consequent outgrowth of public toilets and elaborate public baths.

How important a role soap played in this early bathing fetish is not known. The true discoverer of that magical reaction between grease and leach is still unknown. Assyrian, Egyptian, and Hebrew manuscripts fail to make irrefutable mention of soap, although many herbal concoctions were used in medicine, bathing and personal care. Archaeologists believe that Egypt's legendary Queen Nefertiti used facial masks of honey, milk, and flower pollen to cleanse her pores, while into her bath went the oils of eighty herbs and fruits. It is thought that the Phoenicians may have used soap in bartering with the Gauls around 600 B.C. Certainly, the early Gauls did create a festive hair pomade of goat's fat and beechwood ash. However, the first literary reference to soap, as a means of cleansing person or clothes, is by the Greek physician, Galen, in the second century A.D. Actual soapmaking unquestionably predates this account. A complete soap manufactory was uncovered in the ruins at Pompeii, in southwest Italy, enveloped in 79 A.D. by the lava eruption of Vesuvius.

This has led to speculation that the reaction peculiar to fat and ash was in fact first discovered by the Romans. At Sapo, a hilly area near Rome, the populace sacrificed burnt offerings to their gods. The fat and ash accumulated at the base of the altars, washing down the hillside. Washwomen found this "sapo clay" most conducive to laundering soiled togas, and it only remained for an enterprising chemist to work out the proportions. Whatever the truth of this legend, the name of the product in almost every language derives in part from Sapo: *savon* (French), soap (English), *sapone* Italian), *zeep* (Dutch), *Seife* (German).

With the sacking of Rome, bathing and soap were submerged in the Dark Ages, and the era of the Great Unwashed, with its waves of devastating plagues, began.

During the Middle Ages in most of Europe, bathing was considered the instrument of the devil. A fourth century pilgrim to Jerusalem apparently boasted that she had not washed her face for eighteen years, in an effort to retain the holy chrism of baptism.

At this time baths were taken as a medical prescription, and did not necessarily imply the complicity of soap. More frequently, they were a brew concocted of water and perfume oils or herbal condiments such as camomile, pine needles, or oak bark.

The fragrant spices and herbs brought back by Mediterranean explorers made Italy once more the cosmetic centre of the civilized world. By the eighth century, soap was again being manufactured both here and throughout the Iberian peninsula.

By the thirteenth century, soap had made its way to France, and by the fourteenth, it was established in England, at least for laundry use. The cosmetic pampering of the Continentals was sternly discouraged by the stout-hearted British who placed a heavy excise tax on soap. Nevertheless, by 1700 there were 63 soap companies in London, England alone. Despite this, soap for personal cleanliness was still more a curiosity than a household item. In fact, when A. Leo sent a parcel from Italy to Lady von Schleinitz in 1672, he tucked a note in with the soap, describing in detail how the mysterious product was to be used.

The movement that was to change all this was already nascent. Medical research was sparked by the discovery of bacteria in the late 1600s by Anton van Leeuwenhoek, a Dutch chamberlain who first saw the "wee beasties" in a raindrop through his home-ground lenses. More than a hundred years later, the bacteriological studies of Louis Pasteur led to the theory that microbes were the cause of disease. This fostered a concern with cleanliness as a means of eliminating disease-producing germs.

The so-called hygienic movement was slow to attract adherents. The scientific and medical community, though skeptical, succumbed long before the general populace could be convinced of the merits of personal cleanliness. For too long, the bath had been associated with an icy cure endured by the sick. Now even the healthy were encouraged to bathe, not only often, but with warm water, and with soap.

Christian condemnation of bodily pleasures and the Victorian ethic of modesty were rocked by the seemingly sinful "soap bath." A treatise from 1880 describes at length the innovative technique, which went far beyond the usual perfunctory cleansing of the parts that showed. The bather was directed to stand unclad before a basin of hot water, lathering the body quickly from head to foot. Drying and dressing are mentioned but rinsing must be assumed. The use of soap on a regular basis was discouraged, but devotees were assured that a soap bath could be undertaken at any time of year. It is difficult for our shower-a-day culture to fully grasp the revolutionary nature of such advice, but only in the last fifty years

TAYLOR'S CONGO SOAP

has the soap bath been taken for granted.

The tenets of the hygienic movements, however, were empty words to the early settlers of the New World. The harsh climate discouraged regular bathing for at least half the year. In early French Canada, the celebration of St. Jean Baptiste heralded not only the coming of summer, but also the first bath of the season. The nearest river or lake had to suffice as washbasin, with soap a seldom-seen luxury. Stones pounded dirt from soiled laundry while sand and lye-water scrubbed the cabin clean.

As communities edged inland, even securing a supply of fresh water posed a problem. In Saint John, New Brunswick, as in many villages, water was peddled door-to-door at a cost of a penny a pail, up until 1851. This alone would deter most self-indulgent soaking.

With the addition of livestock to the homestead, soapmaking became part of the annual cycle, an extension of the axiom that he who wastes not, wants not.

14   In the fall, when the animals were slaughtered, the fat was stripped off and rendered in the large cast-iron kettle. The air was cool enough that the strained, hardened tallow would stay sweet until spring. When the snow melted, and the kettle was released from its duty as a sap evaporator, it was pressed into service as a soap boiler. The melted fat was boiled with lye-water leached from the winter's ashes to produce a harsh jelly-like soap. Stored in a wooden barrel and brought indoors by the crockful, this strong soft soap washed clothes and floors and occasionally rendered a foul-mouthed child temporarily speechless.

Commercially, soapmaking in Canada was introduced during early colonization. In 1674, the Intendant of New France, Jean Talon, granted the right of soap manufacture to Nicholas Folin, who saw potential in the oils of porpoises and sea lions. The scarcity of such oils, however, together with Folin's lack of experience, doomed the venture to failure.

Soap manufactories sprang up in most large villages around the end of the eighteenth century. Although independent homesteaders continued to make their own soap until well into this century, by the mid 1800s many small companies were well established in the soap trade. Very often, the production of candles and soap went hand in hand, sharing as they did the common base ingredient, tallow. Householders could obtain finished soap in exchange for the fat collected house to house in soapers' wagons. In remote or rural areas, homesteaders could sometimes trade their potash (a plentiful by-product of clearing the land) for the precious hard bar soap.

These early soapmaking ventures were often of a transitory nature. John Carmichael in his *Treatise on Soapmaking (1810)*, laments the lack of practical printed matter on the soapmaster's art. As a result, inexperienced tradesmen set up in business, enchanted by the seeming simplicity of the process and the lure of easy profit. Carmichael emphasizes the complex responsibilities of the master soaper. Besides an intricate knowledge of the process itself, the master had to understand his ingredients, judging accurately the strength and quality of the lye and its reactions. A sound business sense was no less important, since the excise system was complex and material sources often corrupt. His treatise goes to great lengths to outline methods of testing alkaline salts before buying, since suppliers (kelp burners and barilla makers) often attempted to defraud soapmakers by cutting their product with sand.

Even the fats sometimes came from surprising sources. D.E. MacIntyre recounts in *Prairie Storekeeper:*

No matter whether the butter was good or bad the price was the same to everyone, for any woman would have been insulted if her butter was downgraded. And if I sold it, I was supposed to sell it at the same price I paid for it. Much of it was un-saleable and I packed this kind into butter tubs and shipped it off to soap factories in Winnipeg.

The quality of early soap depended largely on the other main ingredient, lye. In this country, it was made primarily from potash. Only the master soapmaker could produce consistently fine soap from the highly variable potash lye. LeBlanc's discovery in 1790 of the process for producing soda ash from brine not only made inexpensive alkali readily available, but reduced the uncertainty of the trade, paving the way for the large-scale manufacture of soap.

The French chemist Eugène-Michel Chevreul demystified soap in 1823 when he showed that saponification was a chemical process splitting fat and lye into soap (the alkali salt of fatty acids) and glycerine (which he named).

In 1840, Darling and Brady set up a soapworks in Montreal. As contemporary manufacturers of industrial cleansers, they are the oldest soap concern in Canada to continue to function as independent soapmakers. The outgrowth of a tallow candle business, their soap was boiled in thousand-pound batches in iron kettles. The huge soap blocks were cut with piano wire into bars for their first customers who stood in line on St. Urbain Street to buy it.

Within a few decades most Canadian centres nurtured their own independent soap manufacturers, and only rural families continued to make their own. A pioneering venture in the Canadian West was Beaver Soaps Limited of Winnipeg, Manitoba. In 1875 the Royal Soap Company was founded in St. Boniface, Manitoba; in 1878 William Strachan began soap manufacture in Montreal; in 1884 the Ganong Brothers in New Brunswick formed the St. Croix Soap Company; and a short time earlier Dingman, Stickney & Company went into business in Toronto.

Among these independent soapmakers was John Taylor & Co., a small Canadian concern which well reflects the course of soap manufacture in Canada since the end of the last century.

Its founder, John Taylor, set himself up as a wholesale merchant in Toronto in 1865, having immigrated to Canada from England eleven years earlier at the age of fourteen. Goods at this time were sold in bulk and were associated with the store which sold them, rather than the manufacturer. Through his business, Taylor met George Morse of Morse Soaps who was looking for a partner in his production of soap, candles and lard oil. Soap was quickly passing from a luxury to a necessity, and, being a man of foresight, Taylor joined Morse's venture. After a decade of learning the trade, he bought the business, renamed it John Taylor & Co. and concentrated on soaps and perfumes alone.

In England, at about the same time, W.H. Lever was making and selling a new soap with a high proportion of palm kernel oil which lathered more easily than the traditional tallow base. At this time, soap was sold in long anonymous bars, but Lever gave his product a name, Sunlight, which he registered. He then cut and wrapped the bars in distinctive blue and yellow packs and built up a demand by advertising. Lever developed and applied the basic principles of large-scale marketing and mass production with resounding success. In a decade, he was at the head of his field. Across the Mersey River from Liverpool, he built Port Sunlight, a model town for the employees of his huge factory. Before long he had begun an ambitious expansion programme into Europe, America and the British Colonies.

Meanwhile, in Canada, firms like John Taylor's were doing well, packaging and selling their own brand names. Innumerable variations were offered on the simple lye-fat concoction. Eaton's Fall and Winter Catalogue of 1890-91 lists no less than 46 different soaps. The five major companies, Colgate, Morse (Taylor), Albert, Pears and Bailey, all advertised their own brands of the popular oatmeal, glycerine, and Castille soaps. Among the mundane carbolic and fuller's earth soaps are some fascinating labels: Colgate's Turkish Bath, Albert's Sea Foam, not to mention Bailey's Self-Washing, Cyclone, and Electric Soaps. The predisposition to perfumes was obviously assumed by the large assortment of floral offerings, including elder flower, heliotrope, sweet briar, and white clematis. At a time when a teacher earned $400 a year and milk cost five cents a quart, a bar of Colgate's Cashmere Bouquet was rather costly at twenty-five cents.

At this time, advertising was in its infancy. Soap manufacturers were among the first to brand their goods and extol their virtues to the public. Up until the end of the nineteenth century, advertising had only been associated with circuses and the more questionable patent medicines. In the 1880s however, soap manufacturers began to distribute "hand-out" cards. Carrying little more than a picture and the name and slogan of the company, these colourful tokens clearly associated the product with the manufacturer rather than the retailer.

Two British firms, Lever and Pears, led the way in periodical advertising in the last decade of the nineteenth century. The memorable Pears' slogans set the mode for soap advertising: "Good morning, have you used Pears' Soap?" and "He won't be happy till he gets it." From the beginning, soapmakers used a ploy to sell soap which, though well-worn, has yet to lose its appeal. For every twelve wrappers from a six-cent Sunlight twin bar, a "useful paperbound book" could be had. John Taylor offered, for twenty-five Eclipse wrappers, "the much admired Art Picture 'After the Bath,' designed especially for us." For an extra dollar the print came complete with gilt frame. In 1900 Taylor promoted Gold Soap by burying gold coins at random in the laundry bars. After several complaints from retailers that holes were being poked in the soap, the courts ruled that Taylor was guilty of running a lottery, and the gimmick was promptly discontinued.

That same year, Lever built a soap manufactory in Toronto and began producing Sunlight soap for Canadian consumption. As an incentive, the British firm was given land tax-free. John Taylor, whose soaps were the largest selling in Canada and who exported to the United States and the Caribbean, protested against the impact such a concession would have on native Canadian businesses. Although the city fathers gave his business equal exemptions, the first soap multinational soon confirmed Taylor's fears.

With a strong parent company in England, Lever began a national periodical advertising campaign with which smaller native concerns could not compete. In the first two decades of this century, Lever absorbed, one by one, the major Canadian soap industries: Pugsley, Dingman & Company Limited (formerly Dingman, Stickney & Co.) of Toronto in 1906; William Strachan of Montreal in the same year;

and in 1911, Royal Crown of Western Canada.

The Industrial Revolution of the late eighteenth century had contributed to the growing demand for soap by popularizing cheap cotton clothing which required more frequent washing. Together with the impact of the hygienic movement and an increasingly solvent working class, this stimulated soap production, which in turn, gradually put pressure on the supply of fats and oils. Tallow depended on farming while the oil seeds came from tropical plantations: both unpredictable sources. Besides the demands of accelerated growth within the industry, soap manufacturers faced competition for these raw materials from a rapidly expanding margarine industry.

Lever moved early to control its lines of supply by purchasing oil mills and seed plantations. This foresight made Lever relatively immune to a raw materials' shortage in 1906 which hit the small competitors hard.

In 1909, the world-wide problem of adequate oils seemed solved, however, with the development of the hydrogenation process, whereby inferior oils could be transformed into hard soap stock. In 1914, Lever Brothers built a hardening unit in their Toronto branch to make artificial tallow. Besides allowing flexibility in raw materials, it encouraged greater use of domestic products, particularly fish oil from British Columbia and whale oil from Labrador.

Small concerns could not afford such a process and continued to rely on traditional raw materials. Despite this, John Taylor of John Taylor & Co. was a major force in Canadian soapmaking until he died in 1908 leaving his three sons to deal with the rising spectre of conglomerate competition. The company was strong, with thirty-eight medals from international exhibitions and the highest Canadian award for soaps and perfumes in 1906. They produced their own dyes, boxed their own products, controlled Dominion Soaps in Hamilton, expanded into the West with a factory in Calgary, and had a working arrangement with an American company in Rochester, New York. In 1911, when annual sales approached half a million dollars, Taylor merged with St. Croix Soaps of New Brunswick in an effort to streamline production.

In the meantime, Lever had been applying pressure on the Taylors to sell, but they resisted. To recuperate from a serious accident, the company president, A.P. Taylor, travelled to Europe, leaving the business fully in the hands of his partner at St. Croix Soaps. When he returned, John Taylor & Co. had been sold to Lever. The former head of St. Croix Soaps became president of Lever's Canadian operations and A.P. Taylor was left to manage the "Taylor Department" at Lever's.

In competition with British interests, both Procter and Gamble and Colgate-Palmolive from the United States entered the Canadian soap market in the early part of this century. Together with Canada Packers, these four are the primary producers of the approximately thirty-three pounds of cleaning products used by each and every Canadian annually.

Justus von Liebig, a nineteenth century German chemist, proposed that a country's soap consumption was an accurate indication of its wealth and civilization. If so, we have come a long way since 1702, when a Jesuit invoice, requesting supplies for one year for three Fathers and two Brothers, included a mere six bars of soap. Almost two hundred years later, an 1898 Eaton's Spring and Summer catalogue itemized a prospector's needs for a year-long trip to the Klondike, including twelve pounds of soap.

During World War I in Britain, the oils and fats industry came under government control in order to guarantee supplies for the soap manufacturers. The object was not to keep the populace clean, but to secure the source of glycerine, a by-product of soapmaking crucial to the explosives industry.

After the war, the soap business suffered a slump on both sides of the Atlantic. The industry reacted by reducing the number of competing brands, with Lever gradually phasing out most of the Taylor soaps.

A.P. Taylor remained with Lever for only a few years until, as a silent partner, he began Soaps-Perfumes Ltd. It wasn't until 1950 that the name Taylor was officially reinstated in the soap industry.

The thirties saw a drastically reduced consumer market as even essentials became luxuries to the unemployed, and many reverted to home soapmaking. In 1936, a special ten per cent excise tax (above and beyond the eight per cent sales tax) was placed on cosmetics and toilet soaps. Laundry soaps were exempt. In the public's mind, clean clothes were a necessity; clean bodies, a luxury. In reaction, John Savage, president of Albert Soaps wrote to A.P. Tayor:

"I suggest it might help if you and I went alone to Ottawa, and laid our case before the Minister. After all, we are the only one hundred per cent Canadians really hurt, and I believe when Colgate, Williams & Jergens, who are one hundred per cent Americans go to Ottawa, they do more harm than good."

As a result of their efforts, the tax on toilet soaps was reduced to five per cent, but remained in effect until the 1950s, when it was dropped altogether. This signified a change both in public affluence and social attitudes toward personal cleanliness.

Other than a brief period during World War II, soap manufacturing moved ahead after the thirties, especially on this continent, where advertising and the hygienic movement took a particularly strong grip. In laundry products, the gradual changeover from hard soaps toward flakes and powders increased as technology developed both the means of producing soap granules and the washing machines in which to use them.

The soapmaking process itself, however, changed little. In the first part of this century, the kettle process was common, with thousands of pounds of ingredients combined in a steel "kettle," three stories high. Still, it was made batch by batch and poured into wooden moulds before cutting into bars, much as John Carmichael described it in 1810. Around 1940, soap engineers and chemists developed a radically new method whereby soap could be produced in a continuous process. The new method was faster and more efficient with greater quality control. The warm soap was whipped as it cooled, then extruded in a continuous oblong which was cut and stamped into bars.

It was shortly before this technological advance that the soap industry experienced its most crucial transformation. Research into soapless laundry cleaners, begun by the Germans during the oil deficiencies of the First World War, was accelerated by the shortage of animal fats during the farming Depression. In 1933, Procter and Gamble introduced North America to the first household synthetic detergent. The new chemical formula was manipulated until 1947 when Tide, the first non-soap heavy-duty laundry product, hit the shelves. It revolutionized the laundry room. Marketed at a time when mass advertising techniques were gaining respectability and refinement, it was received by a prosperous, actively consuming population.

The soap and detergent industry of today is a considerable one. In 1975, world production of cleaners stood at twenty-two million tons, with North America producing and consuming fully one-third of that. In 1976, the United States alone spent $2.4 billion on soaps, detergents and cleaners. It is still a growing industry. From 1972 to 1976, the population growth of western Europe averaged two per cent while the sale of soaps and detergents increased by more than twenty-five per cent. While North America and Western Europe average twenty to forty pounds of cleaners per capita, Asia's average annual consumption remains at about two pounds per capita, an obvious potential market. While soap still accounts for seventy-eight per cent of the washing products used in Asia, the statistics are reversed in the western world where synthetic detergents represent eighty-five per cent of the total North American consumption and production.

The new chemical base of cleaning products has shifted the source of supply from unmanageable nature to the predictable security of the laboratory. The benefits to households with hard water cannot be underestimated, nor can the industry's claim that natural fats and oils can no longer supply the enormous demand for quick-dissolving, fast-acting, pleasant-smelling washing products.

But the vast chemical industry also creates toxic wastes: in Ontario alone, industry produces fifty million gallons of chemical effluent annually. It is estimated that the quantity of dangerous wastes is increasing by five to ten per cent every year. Our environment is even now suffering from the heavy phosphate concentrations of early synthetic detergents. The standard of living enjoyed by the Western world is undeniably high, but it has a price. For some, that cost is too great.

The past decade has seen a small but definite movement away from the consumerism that marked the decades following World War II. Going back to the land has been a metaphorical as well as a physical drive, reviving an interest in doing for oneself. As much as soapmaking was an integral part of the pioneer homestead, turning waste products to good use, it now becomes one more element of the conserver society.

2 Nature's Lathers

The fair maid who, on the first of May
Goes to the woods at the break of day
And bathes in the dew from the hawthorn tree
Will ever after handsome be.

— *Old Nursery Rhyme*

Long before grease and ashes were combined to make soap, there existed natural lathers. A surprising number of plants contain saponin, a substance which, when wetted, yields soap-like suds. Neither a fatty acid nor an alkali, saponin has yet to divulge its composition to the chemist.

Although many species of saponaceous plants exist, few supply the material in appreciable quantities. To extract the saponin, the plant part must be crushed, boiled in alcohol, and strained while still hot. As the solution cools, the lathering agent separates in flocs. This white crumbly powder sudses easily in a water or dilute alcohol solution. Besides its widespread application in cosmetics and soap-making, saponin is often the foaming agent used to produce a "head" on beer and other effervescent beverages.

Probably the best known saponaceous plant, and the most commonly used commercially, is soapbark *(Quillaja saponaria)* an evergreen shrub of the rose family, native to the Andes. Its lathering inner bark is often included in hair tonics and shampoos, besides being an efficient emulsifier. Medicinally, it is also used as a diuretic, as an expectorant for chronic bronchitis, and as a local anaesthetic.

Like the Chilean soap tree, most of these saponaceous plants are tropical. A select few, however, are native to Canada, and others adapted to the harsh Northern climate along with the early settlers.

Saponin was first observed in a plant common to Canadian roadsides, especially in the eastern provinces. Identified as *Saponaria officinalis,* it is also commonly known as latherwort, soapwort, bruisewort, chimney pink, and the familiar Bouncing Bet. Introduced to Canada with pioneering immigrants, it has long been used as a natural soap, particularly in the washing of rare museum fabrics.

When the dense, spiky clusters of pink and white flowers are in bloom (July to October),

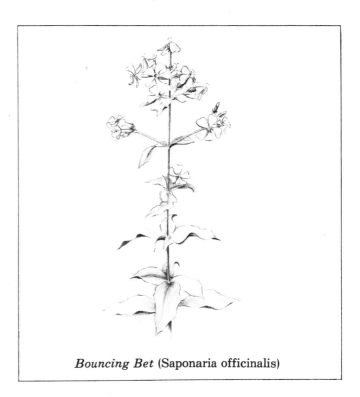

Bouncing Bet (Saponaria officinalis)

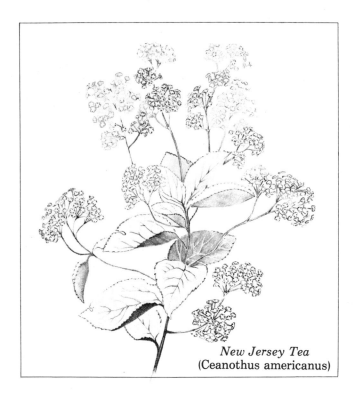

New Jersey Tea
(Ceanothus americanus)

the roots may be dug and crushed in water. The slightly gummy, soapy foam which results is especially good for washing wool, as well as silk, to which it transmits a unique lustre. All parts of this plant will lather to some degree.

Related to *Saponaria officinalis,* which stands one to three feet tall, is the *Saponaria ocymoides,* a trailing perennial less than one foot high, with pink flowers in flat-topped clusters.

Although native to the coastal regions of the United States, the Sweet Pepperbush can be cultivated in the more temperate regions of Canada. A hardy species of the White Alder family, this deciduous shrub sometimes grows up to ten feet. Found mostly in swamps and sandy soils, it produces erect racemes of fragrant white blossoms during late summer. The dense slender spikes of flowers can be used as a soap when rubbed in soft water.

Lamb's-Quarters, *Chenopodium album,* that ubiquitous summer weed, not only provides good salad fare, but helps to wash up afterwards. While its leaves are known as a nutritious vegetable and its seeds ground for flour, its roots, when fresh and crushed, can be used as a mild soap substitute. Also known as pigweed, it is a member of the Goosefoot Family. Ranging from a few inches to more than three feet in height, the first shoots in early spring provide the best lather. As well, the leaves, when crushed between wet palms, emit a foamy substance which, despite the vivid green, effectively cleans the hands after a day in the garden.

An excellent lather can also be made from the flowers of New Jersey Tea. Officially known as *Ceanothus americanus,* it is a member of the Buckthorn Family, which includes the wild lilac, buckbrush, and soapbloom. Although native to the Pacific coast area, only a few are hardy in the North. A low woody shrub, it grows in the dry open woods of southern Ontario and in the Prairies, producing flowers

Sweet Pepperbush
(Clethra alnifolia)

Lamb's Quarters
(Chenopodium album)

from June to August. Sheltered among broad leaves, these dense panicles of white flowers lather admirably when crushed and rubbed with water.

Generally associated with the deserts of the southwest United States, some species of *Yucca* are hardy enough to withstand Canadian winters. A member of the Lily Family, and a North American native, the *Yucca filamentosa* or Adam's Needle can be found in the Great Lakes region from July through September. Growing to a height of almost twelve feet, its flower stalk rises from stiff, sword-shaped leaves edged with fine white threads. The white or violet cup-like flowers resemble enlarged Lily of the Valley in clusters along the length of the stalk. It is the root of this formidable plant which yields saponin when cut, mashed, and rubbed vigorously in water.

Although not normally found north of the forty-ninth parallel, there are at least two other plant groups traditionally used as soapy substitutes. The Buffalo Gourd of the Pumpkin Family *(Cucurbita foetodossima)* yields an inedible fruit which can be ground up raw and soaked in water to produce a cleansing medium.

Likewise, the Amole or Soap Plant is a bulbous herb of the Lily Family, growing primarily in the midwest area of North America. This *Chlorogalum pomeridianum* provides a lathery soap by crushing the heart of the plant's bulb.

While it is doubtful that any of these herbaceous saponins will ever replace that lathering bar by the sink, a knowledge of them might prove useful at a time when living off the land means just that.

Adam's Needle
(Yucca filamentosa)

3 Soapy Alchemy

Molecular caterpillars and their synthetic relations

The definition of soap is simple: the combination of fats or oils with an alkaline base, to produce a substance which cleans.

How the substance cleans is less obvious. The process is twofold, with soap's ability to remove dirt dependent on its efficiency first as a surfactant (surface-active agent), then as an emulsifying (suspensive) agent.

Despite its reputation to the contrary, water is not very good at making things wet. The tiny droplets, being strongly attracted to one another, have a tendency to coalesce into spheres, the shape which has the smallest surface area for a given volume. This mutual attraction of water molecules is balanced by surface tension which prevents further shrinking. The water is, therefore, inhibited from coming into full contact with either the dirt or the surface being washed. One of the most important functions of soap is to break up these molecular bonds, reducing the water's tension and thus enabling it to spread and evenly wet the object. As such, it is known as a wetting agent or surfactant.

After accelerating the wetting process, the peculiar chemical make-up of soap enables the soap molecule to work as an emulsifying agent. A soap molecule looks something like a caterpillar, with the head being *hydrophilic* or attracted to water. The segments of the body, a chain of CH_2 groups ending in a CH_3 tail, are attracted to oil and are water-repellant or *hydrophobic*. As a result, the soap molecule, with its head soluble in water and its tail soluble in greasy dirt, forms a link between the dirt and water. The dirt is dislodged by mild agitation and the soap holds it in suspension to be flushed away.

In any washing solution, enough soap must be present to emulsify all the dirt. If not, some will remain locked in the surface. Likewise, without adequate agitation and rinsing, the dirt will be redeposited on the object, and the cleaning process defeated.

Not only is the proportion of soap to dirt important, but equally vital is the proportion of fat to alkali in the soap. If too much fat exists, the soap will not have enough emulsifying power left to lift grease from the object being washed. If too much alkali is present, the solution will be too caustic, eating into the surface of the object.

Soap molecules do not always restrict themselves to unions with greasy dirt. When used in hard water, soap reacts with compounds of magnesium, calcium and iron to form new materials which do not dissolve, but appear as a sticky scum ingloriously dubbed "soap curd." Essentially, the soap has been used up as a water softener rather than as a cleaner. It is much cheaper and more effective to use a washing soda or borax as a softener and save the soap for what it does best: removing dirt.

Synthetic detergents were devised primarily to eliminate the problem of soap curd. Although "detergent" literally defines any substance which cleans (including soap), through popular usage it has come to mean soapless, synthetic cleaners. Detergents wash in much the same manner as soaps, although they are synthetically derived and not based on a fat-alkali combination. Most contain chemical components called "builders," which are not cleaning agents, but increase the efficiency of the surfactant by counteracting water hardness, and by improving emulsion.

Although synthetic detergents have eliminated soap curd, they have precipitated other problems. The most common builders in synthetic detergents have been phosphate compounds. While phosphates help detergents work better, they also render the growth cycle of marine plant life more efficient. The use of detergents has expelled tons of phosphates directly into the water system, stimulating growth of water plants and algae. Such accelerated growth and decay uses up the water's oxygen supply, killing fish, and speeding the degeneration of lakes and streams. This un-timely death due to over-fertilization is known as eutrophication. In 1972, the Canadian Government Specifications Board stated that, "Because of the concern over pollution due to the phosphate content in some detergents, it is recommended that wherever possible soap should be used in areas of soft or medium hardness of water, or where water softeners are used."

Soaps, too, are toxic to marine life when in high concentrations. However, such density is rarely found. Bacterial decomposition occurs rapidly and its by-products are not nearly so nutritious for plants as are the by-products of detergent breakdown.

Heavy-duty detergents often contain twice as much builder as surfactant. Essentially, the manufacturer is creating a product which will function under the worst conditions, even though the majority of users never require its full potential. Government tests show that this overkill can backfire. A variety of builders were substituted in a standard detergent formula, which was used in water ranging from hard to soft. When used in water with a hardness level of 135 parts per million or less of dissolved minerals (i.e. the hardness of water used by more than sixty-five per cent of the Canadian population), phosphate builders in concentrations above five per cent actually lowered their cleaning efficiency with some fabrics.

Before this decade, phosphate builders made up twenty-eight to sixty-six per cent of most detergents. When the Canadian government was considering lowering phosphate levels, in the late 1960s, the industry reacted violently, claiming cleanliness standards would be set back twenty years.

Despite industry pressure, in August 1970, the Phosphorous Concentration Control Regulations of the Canada Water Act limited the phosphorous content of home laundry detergents to twenty per cent phosphorous (P_2O_5) or 8.7 per cent by weight. They were further reduced in January 1973 to five per cent (P_2O_5) or 2.2 per cent by weight. Although this reduces detergent phosphate effluent by eighty per cent of pre-1970 levels, the law excludes automatic dishwater products, bleaches, and industrial detergents. The Environmental Protection Service of Environment Canada regularly tests a large number of cleaning compounds for phosphate concentration and will provide a list of the results on request. (See page 127.)

Although sodium tripolyphosphate is still the leading detergent builder, with the enforcement of limited phosphates, detergent manufacturers have been experimenting with other builders, such as NTA (sodium nitrilotriacetate). A special task force on NTA health hazards reported in 1977 to the International Joint Commission conference on the Great Lakes Water Quality Agreement, that NTA constitutes no obvious environmental hazard. In the United States, however, the industry has voluntarily discontinued using NTA pending further study of its environmental and health effects. Many other builders such as citrates, carbonates and silicates are added to detergents, with manufacturers choosing their own phosphate substitutes. Government testing and regulation come only after the fact. In Canada, a new chemical must be registered with the authorities but marketing is permitted immediately upon notification. Many other countries have enacted a waiting period which, in the United States, can be up to six months.

Besides builders, synthetic detergents contain chemicals which whiten clothes, protect washing machines against corrosion, stabilize and suppress suds, as well as containing enzymes which break down the protein structures of certain difficult stains.

Many consumers are encouraged to find that virtually all detergents today are biodegradable. The word has an environmentally safe ring to it, but do not be deceived.

Until a decade ago, detergents contained a foaming ingredient (alkyl benzene sulphonate) which did not break down under normal bacterial action, causing unsightly foam on local water bodies. Prompted by a public outcry, manufacturers willingly substituted a new foaming substance (linear alkylate sulphonate) which decomposes readily, thus eliminating the visible pollution. Although biodegradability reduced the immediate health hazard, detergents retained a high proportion of builders which broke down to their component parts faster but were no less damaging.

In Canada, there are no standards defining soaps for personal care other than those applied by individual companies. Depending on the ingredients, such soaps are considered either cosmetics or drugs, and in either case fall under regulations of the Food and Drug Act.

Toilet and deodorant soaps are cosmetics and must abide by the Cosmetics Regulations; medicated soaps are drugs and are subject to the Drug Regulations of the Act.

Basically, these regulations require a soap manufacturer to print his name and address on all packaging, as well as the identity of the product either in terms of its generic name or its function. No claims regarding its formulation, manufacture or performance can be made unless validating evidence can be produced.

As of the beginning of 1978, the Consumer Packaging and Labelling Act requires manufacturers to file with the Department of Health and Welfare a list of ingredients and their concentration in the product. Evidence of the safety of a cosmetic, under recommended or customary conditions, must be submitted on request to government officials, who can prohibit its sale. A cosmetic presenting an avoidable hazard cannot be marketed unless adequate directions for safe use are included on the label. "Avoidable hazard" includes the threat of injury to the health of the user that can be predicted from the composition of the cosmetic or the toxicology of its ingredients.

Medicated soaps must be both safe and effective, with the government empowered to demand evidence of both from the manufacturer. New ingredients may be considered to be New Drugs and an acceptable New Drug Submission is required before the product is put on the market. Hexachlorophene is an example of a drug severely restricted in cleansing formulae. Products containing less than 0.75 per cent may still be sold as cosmetics while a greater concentration is available only by prescription.

Deodorant and anti-bacterial bars contain chemicals incorporated to reduce the number of bacteria on the skin and thus minimize body odours. After their introduction in the mid-sixties, it was discovered that some people were photosensitive to the substances. In other words, after using such a soap, exposure to the sun caused an allergic reaction which ranged from mild to those requiring hospitalization. Between 1960 and 1962, one of these chemicals called tetrachlorosalicylanilide (TCSA) produced an estimated 10,000 cases of photosensitivity in England. That particular chemical was removed from the market. In 1968, the Canadian government requested manufacturers to discontinue the use of another chemical additive, bithional, due to reports of contact photodermatitis.

Dermatologists generally agree that such chemical additives are at best unnecessary. The germs that are killed will be replenished within two or three hours, and they are not what cause odours in the first place.

Besides anti-bacterial soaps there are also "beauty bars" which purport to eliminate that "soap film" and get you "cleaner than soap." Actually, these are not true soaps, but combine soap and synthetic detergent characteristics.

Although most complexion soaps exist on the premise of softening the skin, the actual process of cleansing counteracts that tenet. As described at the beginning of this chapter, soap molecules suspend oils in the water; they do not discriminate between foreign oils and natural skin oils. In removing dirt and debris, soaps also abrade the top dead layer of skin, and are therefore drying and potentially irritating.

When commercially manufactured, soaps contain much more than the traditional combination of fats and alkali. Antioxidants, optical brighteners, stabilizers, colour, and scent are all considered essential by the industry. Unfortunately, such addtives can have unpleasant side effects, most often of two varieties. An ingredient can cause an immediate reaction in the form of a primary irritation, which would affect anyone using the product. Alternatively, it can cause an allergic reaction in those persons sensitized to the particular ingredient. When applied in concentration, irritants can produce a skin rash, which decreases or is eliminated entirely when the irritant is added in smaller proportions to a formula. With allergens, however, even a minute amount will set off a reaction in a sensitized user.

Synthetic additives are not alone in precipitating negative reactions. Almost every additive, natural or synthetic, is sure to trigger someone's allergy or irritate some sensitive epidermis. Even the natural essential oils used in many old recipes can cause problems. Among potential photosensitizers are essential oils of bergamot, cedar, coriander, lemon grass, orris root, orange, parsley and yarrow, to name but a few. Cocoa butter and coconut oil may produce a reaction in those allergic to chocolate and nuts. Natural emollients such as lanolin and glycerine are also culprits, along with honey, which may cause reactions in those allergic to pollen.

Although skin irritations and allergic reactions are annoying and uncomfortable, their immediacy makes it possible to avoid a recurrence by isolating and eliminating the offending ingredient. On the other hand, long-term cumulative effects are not obvious, and are therefore potentially more insidious. The toxin gradually builds up over repeated use, with few symptoms, until the small applications prove more devastating than a single large dose. History provides many examples, particularly the lead-laced powders which whitened Egyptian cheeks.

Although many additives, natural essential oils included, are lethal when ingested orally even in small quantities, a poison does not have to be eaten to be effective. Some can be absorbed through the skin. Healthy skin often acts as a barrier, with broken or abraded skin providing passage for potentially harmful ingredients. There are, unfortunately, those additives that are absorbed into the system even through an unmarked epidermis.

Few natural ingredients fall into this category, and those which do, such as lead, have been in use long enough for their ill effects to emerge. The problem with synthetic additives arises from the relative newness of such laboratory creations. These ingredients have so short a history that, despite industry precautions, cumulative effects cannot be accurately predetermined. Testing with animals provides questionable conclusions, since experts will argue with equal fervour either for or against correlating the results with human use.

With allergies on the increase, particularly skin disorders, additives in soaps are potentially the source of discomfort. In *Conquering Your Allergy*, Dr. Boen Swinny recommends that "the sparing use, especially between the legs and under the arms, of a plain white neutral soap is sufficiently cleansing for the bath. Water and hands are quite effective in removing dead skin and the surface accumulations of the day. The simplest practices of hygiene and cleanliness are the best."

In producing your own soaps, you can at least control the amount and nature of the additives, be they chemical or natural. For a list of ingredients, their uses and potential effects, see Glossary of Ingredients, Chapter Nine.

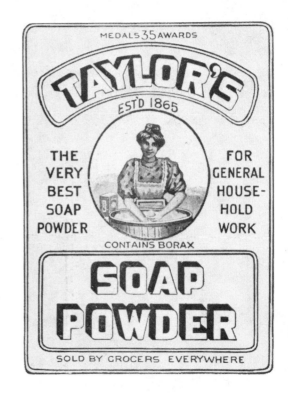

4
Preparations

The soapster's tools and ingredients

While the soapmaking process itself is not complex, a thorough understanding of the basic components will ensure consistent success.

WATER

The most fundamental ingredient is water. Because of the sensitive chemical reaction which occurs, the quality of that water is important. While rainwater is relatively pure, and therefore ideal for soapmaking, hard water contains minerals which can combine with the lye. Insufficient alkali then remains to react with the fat, resulting in failure. The hard water compounds of calcium, magnesium, and iron can be neutralized by adding washing soda, borax or ammonia. It is possible, however, to make the water too alkaline by using too much softener. The amount required varies with the locality and the hardness of individual water sources. More than sixty-five per cent of Canada's population use water below the hardness level of 135 parts per million (of dissolved minerals), and eighty-five per cent use water below 330 ppm.

Although local health officials will analyze your water, there is a satisfactory home hardness test. Make a solution of pure soap in one-half cup of denatured alcohol or wood (methyl) alcohol. Add the soap a little at a time until the solution is as strong as possible without thickening when stored at room temperature from day to day. Select two small identical capped containers. Fill one half-full with distilled water or rainwater. Fill the other half-full with the water to be tested. The amounts must be equal. Using an eye-dropper, add the soap solution, one drop at a time, to the rainwater bottle. After each addition, shake vigorously to produce suds. Continue to add soap solution until enough suds are formed to cover the surface of the water for one minute when the bottle is laid on its side. Record the number of drops used.

Add the same number of drops of soap solution to the bottle of water being tested. If it produces the same suds, the water is soft and requires no additional softener. If sufficient suds do not form, add more soap solution until suds are produced, identical to the rainwater test. The amount of extra soap solution used represents the amount of soap wasted each time that water is used for washing.

For instance, if twice as much soap solution is required to produce equivalent suds, it means that for every cup of soap you add to your washer, a half cup is softening the water, leaving only a half cup to clean the laundry.

To determine the amount of softener to use, experiment with a known quantity of water, such as one quart. Add a small recorded amount of softener to the quart, mix thoroughly, and fill one of the cleaned capped containers half-full with the softened water. Add soap solution in the same quantity as used to form suds in the rainwater, and mix thoroughly. If adequate suds are not yet formed, add more softener to a fresh quart of water. Repeat the process until suds equal to the rainwater test are formed. These results can be related to washing with soap, by multiplying the number of quarts of water being used by the amount of softener required in the test quart. The efficiency of various softeners and their relative cost can be calculated in a similar manner.

LYE

The second basic ingredient in soapmaking is lye. Soapmaking has become more accessible to the homemaker largely through developments in the kind of alkali used. In the early 1800s, the main source of alkaline salts were kelp, a seaweed product, and barilla, a Spanish plant, both of which were burned in kilns to produce ashes. In North America and Russia particularly, potash was used. As timber was cleared for homesteads, the wood was heaped together and burned until the embers dissolved into white ashes. These ashes were boiled with water until reduced to a dry salt, which was converted in a fluxing furnace to a red hot mass to be cooled in moulds.

Even until the end of the last century, rural housewives made their own lye from wood ashes. At first the leach container was simply a hollow basswood stump with a hole augered near the bottom. The lye dripped down a bark-lined trench into a pail. Later, the leach vessel became a permanent fixture in some obscure corner of every homestead dooryard. A fifty-gallon barrel with a hole in the bottom, or perhaps even fitted with a faucet, was raised a few feet off the ground and tilted. A sheet of tin bent to form a trough, or a grooved board, directed the flow into a porcelain pail or stoneware crock.

The bottom of the barrel was stuffed with twigs or stones, then a layer of straw to act as a filter. Burlap bags fitted snugly on top of the straw and up around the edges to isolate the ashes which had been accumulated over the winter and stored in a bark-covered bin. Hardwood ashes were kept separate since they made the best lye, while applewood ashes were especially prized, having a reputation for producing the whitest soap.

When the ashes were compressed to about four inches below the lip of the barrel, a slight depression was made in the centre. The more fastidious homesteader then added about two quarts of lime dissolved in boiling water, to neutralize the salts injurious to soap. Regardless, hot water was always poured on for the first wetting, then came jug after jug of cold soft water. Sometimes it took all day for the water to filter through the ashes, and the first caustic drips to hit the pail.

One pioneer lady, who, as a girl, often had the chore of keeping the leach barrel well-watered, recollects:

I remember this one neighbour. I can still see her clear as day, and this would be more than fifty years ago. She would walk through the dining room, the front room, through the porch and the front door to the ash barrel to pour in the water. I always wondered why she carried that dripping pitcher all the way through the house, instead of going out the back door. I guess it was easier than walking around the house. Goodness knows you had to make an awful lot of trips. It always seemed at first as though you were putting water in and it just disappeared. It took the longest time for that leach to start running.

At first the leach was strong and brown, then weakened as water was added, until all the alkali was extracted from the ashes. The strength of the leach was tested by dropping in a fresh egg or potato. If it sank, the leach was weak and needed boiling down. If it buoyed up high, the leach was too strong. It was ready when the egg floated at about half-mast. A barrelful of good ashes yielded approximately four pails of strong lye, which, together with twelve pounds of fat, produced a barrelful of soft soap.

Athough LeBlanc's discovery of the soda ash process revolutionized the soap industry, it wasn't until the introduction of dry flaked lye that the homemaker was released from the time-consuming and inaccurate process of leaching. Today, lye (also known as caustic soda or sodium hydroxide) is generally made by the action of lime on a boiling solution of sodium carbonate. The resulting flaked lye is both convenient and efficient with the added advantage of producing consistently good results. Be sure to purchase only dry flaked lye.

Lye flakes, despite their seemingly innocuous form, must be used with extreme caution. Being hydrophilic, they attract water where none would seem to exist, and in solution cause acute, painful burns. A flake of lye can mix with perspiration, searing the skin. In this event, rinse at least ten minutes under cool water, or wash with a mild vinegar solution.

Lye should always be handled with care (wear rubber gloves), and kept well out of children's reach. When dissolved in water, lye produces fumes which are as caustic as the solution itself. If inhaled, they can cause a sharp burning sensation in the throat and chest. Be careful to mix the lye-water solution in a well-ventilated area, averting your face to avoid inhaling fumes.

Because of its hydrophilic nature, lye must be kept in airtight containers. If the lye particles stick together, moisture has already sapped some of the lye's strength. Although it can still be used, success is guaranteed only with quality ingredients.

FATS & OILS

While lye and water are fairly immutable components, the fats and oils provide interest and excitement in the soapmaking process. A hundred and fifty years ago, tallow (the rendered fat of cattle) was the preferred base in both home and commercial soap operations. It cools to a hard consistency somewhere between the spongy softness of lard (pork fat) and the brittle hardness of mutton fat. In the early part of this century, the process of hydrogenation was developed whereby inferior oils could be converted into hard soap stock, releasing the industry from its reliance on tallow. Nothing, however, can replace the quality of pure rendered beef fat, and fortunately, it is still practical for the home soapmaker. Most independent butchers will sell large slabs of fat for a few cents a pound. Trimmings are quite a bit of extra work; ask for the solid pockets of fat surrounding internal organs such as kidneys.

To produce clean, white odourless soap, the fats must be fresh or fresh frozen. Once all specks of meat and blood are trimmed, the fat is cut into small chunks, and melted slowly over low heat, preferably in a cast-iron frying pan or casserole. The flaccid morsels shrivel to crisp cracklings, which surface in a fused lump in the light amber oil. Strain the fat through layers of cheesecloth or a sieve, saving the cracklings for the birds. Each pound of untrimmed beef fat yields at least one cup of strained rendered tallow. Pork fat may yield up to twice as much. The cooled hardened tallow can be stored in appropriate measures for soap batches. It can be frozen, but, if well-strained, will stay sweet at cool temperatures for several weeks. Do not store fat where it can absorb strong odours such as onion.

Reclaimed cooking grease can also be used, but some effort is required if good soap is to result. Reclaimed fat is a definite second choice to freshly rendered tallow. The association of homemade soap with harsh, smelly, yellow bars can be blamed at least partially on using recycled kitchen fats without processing them first for soapmaking.

Beef and pork fats should be stored separately to ensure an acceptable tallow content. Lard alone does not produce sufficiently hard soap by the method described in Chapter Five. When enough reclaimed cooking fat has been collected, it must be "washed," by adding an equal amount of water and bringing to a boil.

Remove from the heat and add one-quarter as much cold water to the mixture. This will cause the dirt, lean meat, salt, and impurities in the fat to precipitate. As it cools, the fat will form a layer on top of the water and impure ingredients. When the fat has hardened, scrape the impurities from the bottom of the cake and repeat if necessary.

To further improve reclaimed fats for soapmaking, they can be boiled for ten minutes in twice the quantity of water to which one tablespoon of salt or alum has been added.

Reclaimed grease may contain unpleasant odours which can taint the finished soap. Potatoes cooked in the grease will absorb most of the smells. This should be done before "washing" the fat. Tallow which is rancid or smells a little "off" can also be sweetened by heating it with a lemon or vinegar solution. Two tablespoons of lemon juice or vinegar dissolved in one-half cup water and boiled with one cup fat will improve its character for soapmaking.

Cooking often leaves fats discoloured, which will produce a muddy yellow soap. Even fresh fats, when rendered at high temperatures, will darken. Potassium permanganate can be used to bleach them white again. A few crystals dissolved in two cups of soft water should be added to the same quantity of melted fat. More solution can be added if necessary. The bleached fat will harden as it cools, forming an easily removed cake on top of the water.

Although all of the above methods can be used to improve discoloured, odorous fat, nothing will bring them to the standard of fresh, clean tallow, properly rendered.

Tallow soap alone is very hard soap which will not lather as well as commercial face soaps. To produce a finer soap, vegetable oils must be added. By themselves, these oils do not generally produce a good hard soap, but in combination with tallow, both are enhanced. A mundane vegetable or salad oil can be used, as well as the more expensive olive, coconut, corn, and safflower oils. Chapter Six outlines in detail the various uses and effects of oils in soapmaking.

EQUIPMENT

As far as equipment is concerned, very little is required for making soap at home, and most of it is already in the kitchen. As mentioned earlier, the ten-gallon cast-iron "cooler" was used by homesteaders for soapmaking. Cast iron will, however, tend to discolour the soap, unless very well seasoned. Because of the caustic nature of the lye and the soap itself before saponification is complete, the choice of equipment is important. Soapmaking utensils should be kept expressly for that purpose: once lye has etched the surface, it becomes difficult to clean, creating a potential health hazard.

The container for the lye solution will suffer the most wear. Glass, plastic, unchipped enamel or stoneware may all be used. Be prepared to replace them periodically as lye will mark the interior surface of any material.

The container for the actual soap mixture should be of glass, enamel, stainless steel or stoneware. Be sure that it is large enough to hold the recipe easily. A shallow bowl will cool and set more quickly, necessitating close supervision to prevent the formation of crusty edges. Too deep a bowl will require much longer to cool. A large stoneware (three-quart) bread-baking bowl will easily accommodate the largest batch, while small tests can be made in four-cup glass measuring cups.

The stirring stick or spoon should be wooden or plastic. The lye will actually eat away the wood, requiring frequent replacement. If the caustic power of lye was not appreciated before, the spoon's condition should be proof enough.

Measuring spoons for the dry lye flakes can be plastic or stainless steel. Measuring cups should be glass or heat-resistant plastic. *Never use tin or aluminum products for soapmaking.* They will turn black and the surface will pit and corrode as the metal reacts with the lye.

A pair of rubber gloves is a wise investment before transforming the kitchen into a soapery. A pad of newspapers on the counter is another worthwhile precaution. Although the process is simple, the ingredients are caustic and accidents can happen, even to the experienced soapmaker. One grandmother, using the old-time soft soap method, had graduated from the outdoor kettle to boiling it on her electric stove. One day she decided to give a batch an extra minute or two on the burner. When she turned her back, it bubbled to the rim of the pot. Grabbing the handle, she made for the sink.

There must have been some soap spilled on the floor, because I slipped, lurching forward. The liquid soap slopped all over my open cupboards and into the sink, down the drain. It was good soap all right. The minute it hit those cold pipes it hardened solid as a rock. A plumber had to take the pipes apart right down to the drain in the basement. What a job he had getting out that soap! My left arm was burned by the splashing soap, and by the time I got that mess cleaned up, my right hand was raw from the lye. So accidents can happen. After all those years of making soap, I guess I just thought I didn't have to be careful.

MOULDS

Once the ingredients are prepared and the soapmaking equipment is assembed, an appropriate vessel must be found in which to harden the liquid soap.

For preliminary test batches, almost anything will do. A mould should be fairly regular in shape and preferably of a slightly pliable material. The soap will shrink as it hardens, making it easier to remove. Old soap dishes, the bottoms of plastic bottles, wooden boxes, plastic refrigerator containers, glass or enamel baking pans, all make acceptable soap moulds. Open-ended moulds such as plastic cookie cutters can be used if pressed into a slab of neutral coloured clay, plasticine or play dough. Even a stiff cardboard box will suffice.

Before it sets, liquid soap is caustic, so moulds should be dispensable. The saponifying mass will eat through most paint and varnishes and will absorb dyes, so choose a mould accordingly. Before use, it must be completely greased with a thin film of petroleum jelly to act as a separator. This will ease the process of removing the hardened soap and will give it a smooth finish.

Making your own moulds can be a satisfying extension to the soapmaking process, particularly if you plan to consistently produce your own cleansers. Making a mould similar to the grid shown in the illustration minimizes the work of cutting and removal, producing thirty-six standard-sized bars of soap (approximately three ounces each). Essentially, it is a frame with interlocking inserts, open top and bottom. One side is flush while two walls on the other side are extended. To use the mould, it is positioned on a flat panel, flush side down. After the soap is well set, the mould is raised off the

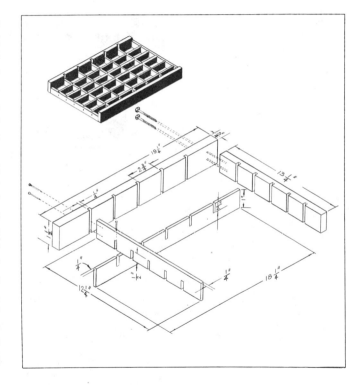

panel and inverted. The bars can then be pushed through the grid and left on the panel to cure thoroughly.

This mould can be constructed of wood or plexiglass. Wood has the advantage of being economical since scrap lumber can be utilized. Fabrication techniques in wood are also more familiar to most budding builders. However, the alkali of the setting soap eats into the wood with time, causing some minor splitting and warping. As well, if left too long in the mould, the soap bars will absorb some natural wood stain on the outer surfaces.

Plexiglass overcomes the discolouration and degeneration of wood, but has its own problems. The smooth surfaces give a fine finished look to the soap, but the mould also scratches easily. Construction must be done with care, preferably leaving adhesive paper intact until completed. Working with acrylics is less familiar, though not difficult. A handsaw with ten to twelve teeth per inch can be used to make cuts. In general, secure clamping, sharp clean tools and straight even strokes will ensure a minimum of friction and smooth cuts. Joints should be cleaned with methyl alcohol before being sealed with a solvent cement. As it is expensive, a novice would be well advised to seek professional guidance rather than waste materials.

Hobby supply shops and mail-order houses carry a wide variety of ready-made moulds designed for use in clear resin casting and candlemaking. Although generally not specified, they can also be used effectively for soapmaking. Metal moulds should not be used, but the plastic and plaster types are ideal. They provide an endless variety of shapes and sizes especially appropriate for gift soaps.

When selecting a mould, remember that soap will absorb dyes. This eliminates the red rubber flexible moulds available from craft houses. The stiff plastic moulds have a limited lifespan as soap moulds since they tend to split and crack with repeated use. When using two-piece candle moulds for three-dimensional soaps, be sure the seams are secure. Candle wax hardens faster than soap, so the shape will be lost unless seams are pinched tight. The recommended taping is not enough: use strong bullclips on three sides to keep seams together, and strengthen potential stress areas with plasticine, play dough or wax. For soap-on-a-rope, a length of washable cord can be doubled, the cut ends wrapped tightly with strong thread for at least two inches, then submerged into the setting soap through the pour hole. Although the soap will set more slowly in a closed mould, it can be removed after twenty-four hours, while still slightly pliable. Be sure to wear rubber gloves. Smooth the seams with your gloved finger or a flat knife and repair any flaws. For a seamless finish, dip the well-cured model into a batch of liquid soap from the same recipe. One or two dippings will put a smooth sheen on the soap without destroying the detail.

You can also make your own three-dimensional moulds, either rigid or flexible, although materials are costly. It is probably just as economical to purchase a ready-made mould, unless you wish to produce an original shape.

In such an event, a number of moulding compounds are available from craft supply houses. They fall roughly into two categories: a dry powder and a ready-mix liquid or paste. The powder is soluble in water, dries extremely fast (two to ten minutes depending on mix) and will reproduce any object in detail, with no harm to the original. (If the original is of a porous material such as plaster, seal before using.) You will need an outside form, such as a plastic margarine container, waxed beverage cup, or cardboard milk container, which is at least one inch larger than the original on all sides. To test the amount of mix required, pour water into the form and submerge your original, leaving a surface exposed as the pour hole. Measure the same amount of water into another bowl. Gradually add an equal amount of moulding compound. A one to one ratio is the strongest proportion although two water to one powder is acceptable. Stir constantly to mix thoroughly then pour into form. Immediately immerse the original in the mix, leaving the top plane exposed. Hold firmly in place until set, which is only a few moments. When set, remove mould from the outside container. Remove the original from the mould, if possible. If the original is larger than the pour hole, use a dull knife to slit the side of the mould cleanly. Remove the original and allow to dry. When using this mould, return it to the outside form, or use elastic bands or tape to hold the parts firmly together while pouring the soap. Although this mould is fine for immediate use, it tends to dry out, shrink, and harden with time. It can be stored for a few days in a tightly closed plastic bag, but should be used mainly for a one-time cast.

Flexible moulds can also be made from liquid latex compounds available from craft supply stores. There are two approaches to fabricating a rubber mould: either it can be built up by brushing on successive layers of moulding material or the material can be cast around the models. The former is appropriate for detailed single moulds of original three-dimensional shapes. Place the original on a wooden base with a border of at least two inches beyond the bottom of the model. If necessary, glue the original to the base for added support. With a small brush, paint the compound over the model and top surface of the wood base. If the compound is too thick, thin with distilled water: it should flow easily. The first coat should be thin, to pick up all details on the original. As each coat dries, apply another, being careful to cover the entire surface each time. A strip of gauze for extra support can be laid on the base or over undercuts between coats. Approximately six coats will be required. This produces a very flexible mould with excellent reproduction, but at only marginally less cost than purchased moulds. Once more, beware of coloured moulding compounds.

The second approach can be used to create flexible original single or multi-bar moulds. The originals can be anything such as hockey pucks or rings of plastic pipe filled with sand, as long as they are heavy enough to stay in place during the process, and of a shape suitable for soap. First, prepare a tray of the desired depth, at least one inch above the tops of the models. The form can be a base plate with clay or cardboard walls, as long as the walls are reasonably strong. Seal the seams with plasticine, clay or wax. Place the original models within the tray, leaving enough space (at least one inch) between objects to provide structural walls. Cover all surfaces with a thin coating of paste wax to facilitate mould removal. Run the moulding compound carefully over and around the originals, being careful not to disturb them. Fill the tray to the top so that the surface is smooth and level. Allow to set and cure. Remove tray and originals, inverting to use. This mould is particularly good for transparent soaps which are very liquid when poured. The same method can be used for either flexible moulding compounds or rigid materials such as plaster.

Once the mould is prepared, fill it with water to determine the amount of liquid soap it will hold. Each recipe includes the approximate liquid yield, so that moulds of adequate volume can be assembled.

WRAPPING

Once it is fully cured, soap may be wrapped for storage. This is advisable with scented bars to preserve their fragrance. After about three weeks, wrap in waxed paper, several layers of white tissue paper, clear plastic wrap, or seal in coin envelopes. Avoid aluminum foil or coloured tissue paper since even cured soap is slightly alkaline.

5 The Test Batch

"There is no such thing as a complete failure in soapmaking...."

— M. Mohr

There are two basic approaches to home soapmaking: the cold process and the hot method. Pioneer housewives using homemade leach produced soap by the hot method as described in Chapter Seven.

The development of commercial lye, however, has led to a safer, more accurate means of making soap at home. This chapter is a step-by-step visual and verbal guide through the cold process, the method of soapmaking most suited to contemporary kitchens.

Above all, cold process soapmaking requires accurate measurement. One disadvantage of this method is that it is difficult, if not impossible, to achieve complete saponification. There is almost always a small but variable amount of free fat which, in quantity, may become rancid, producing foul-smelling brown spots on the soap. On the other hand, free alkali results in a harsh soap. Measure as carefully as possible to avoid either extreme.

Assemble the soapmaking equipment and

EQUIPMENT

Wooden stir spoon
Small bowl for lye solution
Large bowl for soapmaking
Measuring spoons
Measuring cups
Rubber gloves
Rubber spatula
Moulds

NOTE: Never use aluminum or tin utensils for soapmaking, but rather glass, hard plastic, earthenware, enamel, or stainless steel.

MATERIALS

Soft water
Lye flakes
Clean tallow, melted
Petroleum jelly
Additives (optional)

materials according to the checklist on this page. As the test batch will produce approximately three standard bars of soap, select appropriate moulds, capable of holding a total of twelve to sixteen ounces of liquid soap

In one (glass or plastic) container, measure one-half cup cold soft water. After donning rubber gloves, slowly add two tablespoons dry flaked lye, stirring constantly with a wooden spoon until the lye is dissolved. Because of a powerful chemical reaction, the water will quickly heat until it steams. Remembering that these caustic fumes can "catch" in the throat, prepare lye in a well-ventilated area, near an open window, and avert your face. Use extreme caution when handling lye in any form.

In another container, measure one cup melted tallow (beef fat) which has been previously cleaned and strained. Set aside both solutions to cool to lukewarm. Periodically, test the temperature by feeling the outside of the containers. Do not touch the solutions themselves,

1. *Measure lye and stir into cold water.*

2. *Allow lye-water and melted tallow to cool to lukewarm.*

except with a thermometer. The lye must cool to just less than body temperature (90 to 95 degrees F) while the fat should be a bit warmer (120 to 130 degrees F). This stage may take up to an hour: do not rush the cooling process.

While waiting for the solutions to cool, liberally grease the moulds with petroleum jelly and place them where they will remain undisturbed for several hours while the soap hardens. Do not put moulds near heat (i.e. beside a stove) or near extreme cold, as this will affect the setting process.

When the lye-water and fat feel lukewarm, pour the lye slowly into the fat, stirring constantly. When the lye mixes with the fat, the chemical reaction known as saponification occurs. Two distinct components are converted into one new substance — soap. Stir thoroughly to completely emulsify the ingredients, bringing all lye into contact with tallow, so that no free alkali or fat remains.

As it is stirred, the mixture will become

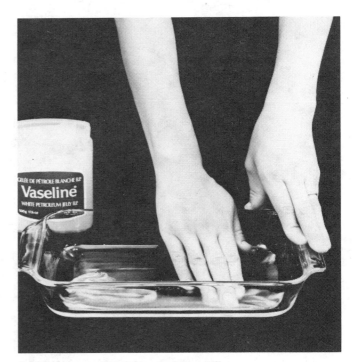

3. *Grease mould with petroleum jelly.*

4. *Slowly pour lye-water into tallow, stirring constantly.*

cloudy, then somewhat grainy. As it approaches the pouring stage, it will thicken like creamy honey or cooked pudding. An electric mixer set on low speed can be used, but hand stirring is just as effective. Check the beaters of any electric mixer before using to ensure they are made of stainless steel.

The amount of stirring required depends on the temperature of the solutions, and can therefore not be predicted. It can be as short as five minutes or as long as an hour. Ten minutes to half an hour is standard.

If the stirring seems to be taking abnormally long, the ingredients were likely too warm. Set the bowl in cold water and continue to stir. The outside edges will tend to cool faster than the inside mass, causing a crust to form. If this begins to happen, remove from cold water and beat vigorously to disperse the lye evenly.

Judging the appropriate time to pour the thickening soap is difficult for the novice, but will improve with experience. Poured too soon,

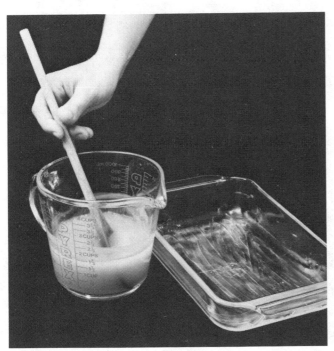

5. *Continue stirring as mixture thickens.*

the soap may separate into a hard bottom with greasy upper layer. Poured too late, the soap will not fill the corners of your moulds and may contain air pockets. Accurately assessing the right moment will produce superior soap.

One criterion for correct pouring consistency is the ribbon test. Take a spoonful of soap mixture, and holding it about two inches above the bowl, dribble a ribbon of soap onto the mass. If the ribbon remains separate and doesn't immediately merge with the rest, the soap is ready to pour into the moulds. Another readiness test dictates that soap is of a proper consistency when the stirring spoon will stand alone in the middle of the mixture.

When thickened, pour the soapy mixture slowly and evenly into the moulds. It should flow easily into the corners, taking the shape of the mould, but should stiffen almost immediately. Scrape out the bowl with a rubber or plastic spatula, and smooth the tops of the bars. It is a good idea to wash all equipment as

6. *When spoon stands alone, mixture is ready.*

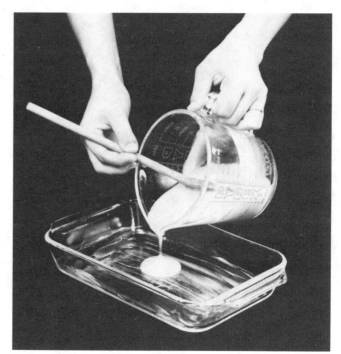

7. *Pour into mould.*

soon as possible, before the soap sets in the bowl. Rinse containers to remove all traces of soap, fat and lye, then wash well in warm soapy water.

The soap will now take an hour or two to set to a firm butter-like consistency. At this stage, if one large mould was used, slice the slab into bars with a sharp knife. If you wait until the soap is too hard, it will not cut cleanly.

The process of saponification is not complete until the soap is fully set. Avoid touching the soap to test its hardness: the alkali is active and caustic until the soap is set.

After twenty-four hours, the bars should be hard and easily removed from the moulds. Soap containing high percentages of coconut oil, lard or vegetable oils may require a longer setting period, up to three days. The time factors will change as well, with the weather and the location of moulds. Although soap hardens in a relatively short time, it should be cured before using. You will no doubt be anxious to

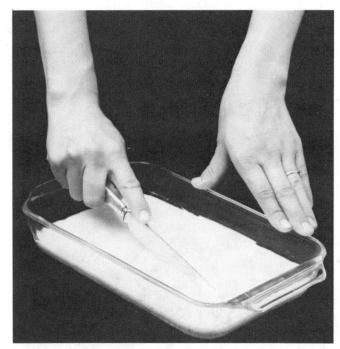

8. *Set two hours, then cut in bars.*

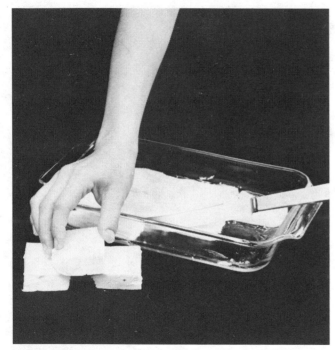

9. *Stack bars brick-like to cure.*

sample your first efforts, but a curing period of up to three weeks will ensure a superior product. In a cool place, stack the bars brick-like with spaces between for good airflow. There may be some shrinkage but the longer it cures, the better it becomes. After three to four weeks in open air, the soap may be lightly wrapped in paper. Hundred-year-old soap is common in museums, and in England, a Tudor tablet is preserved, made in the 1500s.

Commercially, a lustrous finish on soap bars is assured by extrusion from a heated nipple. Before continuous process machinery, the cut bars were treated with a shot of steam which sealed the surface smoothly. In the nineteenth century, when each bar was individually cut and wrapped, it was polished by hand using alcohol and a woolen cloth.

The appearance of your soap will tell a great deal about its quality. The finished bar should be smooth and white, with an even texture and colour throughout. The texture or structure of a soap is partially dependent on its purity. Genuine soaps cooled in frames have a fibrous appearance which becomes more evident when the surface has dried somewhat. Known as "feather," it was considered a merit by early soapmasters. Commercial soapmakers have eliminated this characteristic to a large extent.

The defects in poor quality soap will likewise be evident from its appearance. Most problems stem from poor quality ingredients or inaccurate procedure. The chart on page 67 lists the most common faults, their probable causes and suggested remedies.

If the soap is streaked with yellowish or greyish striations, it is a sign of uneven emulsion. Although the soap is usable, it has not been stirred enough, and may contain pockets of free fat and/or free alkali. It should be used immediately to avoid rancidity.

Soap which refuses to set hard and remains a soft greasy mass contains too much free fat to be usable. Either inaccurate measurement has resulted in an insufficient amount of lye to saponify the fat, or some of the lye has been consumed in combination with hard water minerals.

If the soap has separated to form a greasy soap layer on top of liquid, something.is radically wrong. Either your proportions were grossly inaccurate, or your temperatures were wrong or, more likely, the fat itself was either rancid or impure.

If the soap has separated to form a greasy layer on top of hard soap, you probably poured the mixture too soon into the moulds, before the lye was well emulsified. The greasy layer can be scraped off and the hard soap used, although it may be somewhat alkaline.

If the soap is very hard and brittle, or cracked, there was probably too much lye in the mixture. Too much stirring, a very fast set or exposure to heat, causing rapid shrinkage, will also produce cracks.

Well-made soap should have no strong smell

or taste when licked. If it bites the tongue, there is too much lye. If it smells at all "fatty," either there is free fat which is turning rancid, or the fats were not rendered properly. Tallow which smells at the outset will not improve during the soapmaking process. If the tallow has an odour, it was rendered at too high a temperature, was not fresh to begin with, or contained some meat scraps.

There is no such thing as a complete failure in soapmaking. A flaky residue or greasy layer can be trimmed and the problem corrected next time. Only severe separation into greasy soap and liquid is truly discouraging. Even this can be salvaged, although the inexpensive ingredients may prompt you simply to try again. To reclaim a soap failure, pour the soap (with its liquid) into a kettle along with half its volume of water. Melt and bring to a boil, simmering until it forms stringy ropes from the spoon. If not, add more water, as it can easily be boiled away. Pour into moulds to set.

There has been much discussion recently of pH values in cosmetics, including toilet soaps. pH is a scale of alkalinity and acidity, 7 being neutral. Above 7 is alkaline and below is acidic, with the pH range of normal skin, 5.0 to 6.5. An extremely alkaline soap (above 10), or one with pockets of free alkali, would irritate sensitive or broken skin.

In June 1977, *Canadian Consumer* tested popular toilet soaps and found the bulk to have a pH above 9, somewhat alkaline for normal skin. You can test the pH of your own batch by making a solution of soap in distilled water and measuring it with litmus paper. Litmus is usually available at pharmacies.

John Carmichael describes an early nineteenth century method for determining the acidity or alkalinity of his solution when making lye-water:

Take a parcel of blue flowers of any vegetable, violets for instance, or the blossom of the mallow; beat them with the edge of a knife, and squeeze the juice of it into a teacup; with a small brush or hair-pencil lay over a sheet of white paper with this juice and when dry it is fit for use. All alkalis will turn it green, all acids will turn it red. A combination of acid and alkali to point of saturation will in no way alter the colour because they are neutral, having properties of neither acid nor alkali.

Blueberries produce a fine blue test paper which will indicate general acidity or alkalinity when pressed on a dampened soap bar. Simmer and stir one-half cup of blueberries in one cup hot water until the berries have faded to a pinkish colour and the water is purplish-blue. Brush stiff paper with the blue dye and allow to dry. Cut into strips to test your soaps. A drop of vinegar will turn the paper a deep red, indicating acid, while a drop of lye-water will register brilliant green, possibly even yellow. Since soap is usually mildly alkaline it should register a pale green.

A more accurate acid-base test can also be easily done at home. Purchase a very small quantity of phenolphthalein at your local druggist. As this is a poison, handle with care. Dissolve a few grains (one-eighth teaspoon) in one ounce isopropyl alcohol. Prepare a soap solution by dissolving two teaspoons of soap in five ounces of boiling water. When thoroughly mixed, add a drop or two of the phenolphthalein alcohol indicator. If it does not change colour, it means the soap solution is either neutral or acid. If it turns slightly pink, it is somewhat alkaline, which is acceptable. Deep red indicates the presence of a large amount of free alkali.

The soap which you produce will last much longer than commercial varieties. In the same June 1977 issue of *Canadian Consumer*, small toilet soap bars were subjected to a life test. This consisted of a simulated bathroom cycle in which the bar was soaked, dried, and briskly lathered in hot water. The bar was weighed beforehand and the test was stopped when it was reduced to twenty per cent of its original mass.

Most brands held out for twenty cycles, which translates to three to four weeks of average home use. Homemade bars should last up to twice as long.

Your homemade soap will easily outlive its commercial competitors, and the reason is glycerine. When an oil is saponified, glycerine is a by-product of the reaction. In early manufacture, the glycerine was salted out with the spent lye and thrown away, until a lucrative glycerine industry evolved. Now glycerine is an important by-product of the soap industry. Your own bars, of course, retain this valuable glycerine.

A clear, syrupy, very viscid liquid, glycerine has a strong affinity for water. As a result, homemade soap contains a much higher percentage of water and is considerably less dense than commercial bars. Common tallow soap contains thirty to fifty per cent water while pure coconut soap can contain up to seventy-five per cent and commercial soap as little as ten per cent.

The high proportion of water in homemade soap may lead to sweating and shrinking as it sets, an obvious disadvantage in commercial manufacture. The presence of glycerine, however, also contributes to longevity. Commercial bars contain so little moisture that, when put in water, they absorb it rapidly. This produces a slimy film around the bar and makes for a quick copious lather. It also means each exposure to water washes a large percentage of the bar down the drain.

Homemade soap will not lather as readily, because it already contains a great deal of water and does not soften as quickly on contact. On the other hand, it will not degenerate in the soap dish or dissolve in the bathwater. The greater density of commercial bars causes them to crack and break when well-used, whereas the softening effect of the glycerine maintains the shape of a homemade bar down to a fine sliver, resulting in less waste.

Soap Defects: Causes And Cures

SYMPTOM	CAUSE	PREVENTION
Separation: greasy layer atop hard soap	Liquid soap poured too soon: lye poorly distributed; incomplete saponification	Stir more thoroughly; do not pour until thick and creamy; measure accurately.
Separation: greasy layer atop liquid	Inaccurate proportions; inaccurate temperatures; rancid or salty fat	Follow directions carefully; render and clean fat well.
Soft, greasy soap	Incomplete saponification; too little lye; some lye used up in hard water	Soften water before making soap; measure accurately.
Streaked soap	Too little stirring; uneven emulsion	Pour lye more slowly into fat; stir well; accurate temperatures.
Very hard, brittle soap	Too much lye; fat too hard (mutton)	Measure lye accurately; add lard or vegetable oil.
White residue on hard soap	Too much lye; hard water	Use rainwater; measure accurately.
Cracks in soap	Too much lye; too much stirring; too thick when poured; set too fast	Reduce lye; pour when creamy thick; set at room temperature away from excessive heat.
Soap smells "fatty"	Free fat which turns rancid; odorous fats	Stir well for complete emulsion; correct proportions; render at low heat; use fresh fats; wash fats before use.

6
Hues
& Essences

Variations on the theme

The soap just produced in the test batch is a plain white all-purpose cleanser. With it you can wash your face, your clothes, the floor, or the dog.

There is, however, much more to soap than this. By the addition of oils and essences, fragrances and fillers, the basic properties of soap can be manipulated to serve specific ends.

In the soap industry, the product you have just made is termed "neat soap." Commercially, this base is cooled and processed into flakes or noodles for sale to custom soapers and finishers. These neat soap flakes are produced in several qualities, varying in price according to the raw materials used. They differ in colour from almost pure white to greyish, yellowish brown. Provided that you have taken care in rendering your tallow and exercised accuracy in measurement, you have made a soap base of the highest quality.

The second stage of toilet soap manufacture entails the addition of perfumes, dyes, superfats, and chemical stabilizers, brighteners, and anti-oxidants to the soap base. These are mixed, milled on huge granite rollers to distribute the additives evenly, then compressed and extruded in a continuous shaft to be stamped and wrapped.

Contemporary commercial soap manufacturers rely primarily on synthetic chemicals to produce the strong scents and bright colours indicative of the cosmetic section. Until this century, soaps were lightly perfumed with natural essences, often distilled by the soapmaster himself. Some soaps, notably the $5-to-$10-a-bar brands, still make use of these natural scents. While the elaborate chemical concoctions are not available to the home soaper, the natural additives of the last century are. Although too costly and in too short a supply for large-scale manufacture, these additives still make economic sense for the individual soapmaker.

Installing a distinctive aroma in soap is not

quite as easy as adding a dash of your favourite perfume. While alcohol develops the finer ingredients of a fragrance, soap modifies the scent so as to make it often unrecognizable. Also, too large a proportion of alcohol from the perfume may upset the saponification process.

SCENTS

Essential oils are the best natural means of adding scent to soap. While there are various means of extracting these oils from plants, not all are adaptable to home use. The most expensive and exacting technique of the perfume industry is enfleurage, which takes advantage of a flower's ability to produce and exhale perfume even after it is picked. The fresh, unbruised flower petals are immediately laid on a glass spread with lard and topped with another larded glass pane, so that each flower is sealed in fat. For several weeks, the old petals are removed daily and new ones applied, until the lard is saturated with perfume oil. The fat is then melted and frozen into a pomade, which can be used as is, or agitated in alcohol to dissolve the perfume oil. The alcohol is then removed by distillation, leaving a pure essential oil.

The method most accessible to home soapers is maceration, whereby fragrant flowers are immersed in warm fat which absorbs the essential oil. Since a large quantity of strongly-scented petals is required, they must be both abundant and easily removed. In the spring, fruit tree blossoms are ideal. To transfer blosssoms from the tree to the pot, lay a sheet or blanket beneath the tree and shake the petals loose. This does not interfere with the tree's ability to bear fruit. Timing is important: the flowers cling to the branches until just before they die off. There is a short period during which the fragrant blooms are still at their peak, yet fall easily with a brisk shake. Pick out any twigs, leaves and creatures which may have come down with the flowers. Measure equal amounts of blossoms and fat by volume, then soak the flowers (slightly crushed) in warm fat for at least an hour. Do not boil or scorch the fat, but keep it warm.

The temperature of the fat is important. If simmered actively, the perfume oils will volatilize and escape with the steam. If it is too cool, the oils in the blossoms will not be as readily digested. Ideally the fats should be melted and lukewarm (120 to 140 degrees F) when the flowers are added. Strain before using for soapmaking.

Since the availability of perfumed blossoms is highly seasonal, the soap can be made and stored, or the fat can be frozen for later use. Blossom fragrance, depending on its strength, will be retained in soap for up to six months, particularly if lightly wrapped.

Another method of expressing herbal and floral oils can easily be used at home. Place a shallow enamel pan of hot water over lowest heat. Place a clean cloth across the pan, tying it securely around the edge. Place two pounds of petals on the cloth, and on them, a dish of cold water. Change the water periodically to keep it cool. With a cotton ball, soak up the oil which forms as a scum on the hot water. Squeeze the liquid into a clean glass jar with several layers of cheesecloth stretched across its mouth, and set out for several days. The excess water will evaporate leaving a pure essential oil. Such oils can be stored for long periods in clean amber glass jars with tight lids, preferably in a cool place to avoid rancidity.

A more time-consuming method involves placing selected plant parts in a clean ceramic crock, barely covering with rainwater. Put the crock in the sun and after a few days a filmy scum will appear on the surface. This is the oil: absorb it daily with a cotton ball and squeeze into a dark-coloured glass jar. A piece of netting will keep bugs out of the crock but be careful to bring it in out of the rain.

Some plants are more generous with their essential oils than others, which perhaps explains their price range on the marketplace. One hundred pounds of selected rose blooms are required to produce one-eighth to one-quarter ounce attar of roses. From the same weight of blossoms, lavender yields two pounds of oil, cloves eighteen pounds, and castor beans twenty to fifty pounds.

Any strongly-scented flower, herb, root, or bark will yield its essential oil. Floral petals should be picked early in the morning, selecting only top quality plant parts. Roots and bark must first be reduced to shavings with a plane, garden shredder, or blender. Oils can be extracted using any of the methods described: experiment with vanilla bean, wintergreen, mint, oak bark, and herbs such as sage and thyme.

Approximately one per cent essential oil (varying with the type of oil and its relative potency) should be added to the total soap volume just before pouring into moulds. Without chemical stabilizers, the action of the aklali may change the initial fragrance of your essential oil. The best test is to store a sample bar for at least three months to judge its stability over time and exposure to air.

Certain essential oils are more stable by nature than others. The following oils, whether home-produced or purchased, are the best suited for creating fragrant soaps:

Ajowan oil	Heliotropin
Bois de rose oil	Lavender oil (spike)
Cassia oil	Palmarosa oil
Caraway oil	Patchouli oil
Cedarwood oil	Peppermint oil
Ceylon citronella oil	Peru balsam
Clove oil	Rosemary oil
Eucalyptus oil	Sandalwood oil
Geranium oil	Sassafras oil
Guaiac-wood oil	Thyme oil

Despite its addition at the end of the soap-making process, an essential oil tends to be drained of some of its fragrance by the continuing saponification. Although it entails more work, a truer scent can be obtained by double-batching. Using this method, the soap is essentially made twice. In the first batch, the alkali is used up and saponification completed. After curing, the soap is melted down in a second batch and the essential oil added. Thus the harshness of the soapmaking process is accomplished separately, previously, and does not interfere with the scent.

First, make a test batch of simple soap using twenty per cent olive or coconut oil in the fat. Allow to set until hard (at least three days).

Shave the soap fine using a stainless steel or plastic grater or shredder. Melt the shaved soap with half its volume of water and simmer gently in a double boiler until it is ropy when poured from a spoon. Remove from heat, allowing the mixture to cool slightly. Add the essential oil, (approximately one to one and a half teaspoons depending on personal preference), beating vigorously before pouring into moulds.

Other than perfumes and essential oils, there are additional ways in which to instill fragrance in soap. Synthetic scents used in candle making can be added successfully to the liquid soap. Finely powdered aromatic spices such as cinnamon, cloves, and nutmeg, when mixed with a little oil, can be added to the finished liquid soap just before pouring into moulds. Likewise, pure flavouring essences such as vanilla or almond can be added in small quantities.

Because of the fatty nature of soap, it will absorb scent readily, particularly when freshly made. Spread fragrant dried herbs such as lavender or chopped pine needles on a tray or jelly roll pan. Cover with cheesecloth and set bars of plain soap on top. The delicate scent will be imparted to the soap as it cures.

COLOURS

Due to the chemical nature of soap, colours are much more difficult to secure than scents.

Keep in mind, when experimenting with tints, that *all* colours are darker in the liquid state and will fade somewhat on setting.

Candle dye, being a synthetic compound, will adequately colour soap if added just before the soap is poured into the moulds. It is best to reserve a little of the vegetable oil, mix the candle dye with it, and add this in the final stages of stirring, beating vigorously to distribute the colour evenly. As these dyes are potent, use them sparingly (one-half teaspoon per one cup fat). Food colouring, with the exception of yellow, is not very stable and tends to be bleached and distorted by saponification.

Natural dyes produce fascinating, often unpredictable results when applied to soapmaking. Vegetable colours are highly unstable in the presence of alkali, which will reduce to beige the brilliant greens, reds, blues and yellows of nature. For instance, any attempt to use blueberries to colour soap blue will result in colour changes from the lye. The transformation is remarkable: raspberry or blueberry juice, when added to liquid soap, changes to brilliant blue, then neon green, mustard yellow, bright brick, finally setting to a muddy rose beige. Any attempt to use the vegetables dyes traditionally associated with the fabric arts will meet with less than satisfactory results. Onion skins, which can be used to dye fabrics a sunny yellow, will turn your soap a dismal grey.

It is possible, however, to use powdered spices to colour soap. As with the spice scents, mix a little vegetable oil with the spices before adding to the soap. Beat vigorously to distribute, then pour immediately into moulds. Turmeric, saffron and curry powder produce various shades of cream to peach, depending on the amount used. Cayenne and paprika will create hues from salmon to tangerine. Cinnamon and cloves yield a wide range of beige from caramel to deep chocolate. Since the fragrance of some spices may be objectionable, add only enough to colour but not scent the soap.

In fact, before the age of chemical colours, cocoa and caramel were commonly used to produce a brown soap. Most other colours were produced by means of natural mineral, inorganic pigments. Natural mineral colours, or earth colours, are mined from beds of earth, their colour deriving from the presence in the soil of iron compounds together with varying amounts of clay, chalk, and silica. These have been used since prehistoric times and are quite permanent under normal conditions.

Yellow ochre (iron hydroxide), gold ochre and raw sienna are the earth yellows. Yellow and orange were later produced by cadmium yellow (cadmium sulphides). Red was first achieved with red ochre (iron oxide), then vermilion. Vermilion is a natural mineral called cinnabar, found in Spain, China, and Austria. It has been artificially derived for a thousand years from mercuric sulphide. Natural ultramarine (blue) is a rare and expensive pigment made of ground lapis lazuli, a semi-precious stone. A synthetic substitute has been used since 1826, called artificial soda ultramarine (the chief chemical composition being sodium silicate, aluminum and sulphur). This is the primary ingredient in laundry blueing cakes, which can be crushed and added to soap to dye it blue. Guinet's green, a hydrated chrome oxide, was developed in 1838 in France and used to produce a cool reliable green. Before this, green earth (iron silicate) was used.

Most of these natural inorganic colorants are available through pottery supply houses (see Chapter Eleven). In their pure form, they are potentially harmful if inhaled or ingested, just as particularly sensitive skin may be irritated by direct application. Dissolved in small quantities in soaps, however, they are harmless. Ultramarine blue, umber and the ochres all show no ill effects in use. Chromium oxide greens may result in possible contact dermatitis.

With the exception of synthetic chemical compounds and inorganic tints, the home soap-maker must be content with a subtle colour range. From pale yellow and pinkish buff, tones between pure white and deep brown are easily achieved. In the pursuit of the natural, the hot pinks and avocado greens of commercial preparations may have to be relinquished in favour of earth tones.

Whatever colorant is selected, there are some basic tests to judge its appropriateness for soap. The dye should be very soluble, allowing for even distribution throughout the saponifying mass, without becoming spotty. The colour should be fairly stable when exposed to light and air. This can be judged by preparing a test batch and setting one bar in a light place for several weeks. Store another bar from the same batch in a closed area, then compare the two for colour stability. Above all, the dye should colour only the soap, not the person who uses it or his clothes. Preferably, when lathered, a coloured soap should produce white suds, which indicate that the colour is not bleeding.

FILLERS

Besides colours and scents, master soapers of the ninetenth century often added a variety of fillers. These served multiple purposes, from cosmetic aids to cutting the cost of the soap's manufacture.

Soap made with talc or fuller's earth was once a staple in every soaper's catalogue. This recipe produced a very solid bar with a dull opaque appearance which took on a marble sheen when wet. The silica gave it a smooth silky texture. Other fillers included sand or fine pumice used for heavy-duty cleaning. Bran, cornmeal, maize, and oatmeal were common fillers in cosmetic bars. Gently abrasive, they were purported to stimulate the skin. For hundreds of years, these grains were mixed with honey and used on the face to regenerate a tired complexion.

Ingredients such as grains, egg or vegetable additives can deteriorate even though encased in soap. To prevent or at least delay degeneration, add a small amount of the natural antioxidants, wheat germ oil or vitamin E oil (for external use).

Paraffin and beeswax were at one time used to extend the soap and make it softer to the touch. Many early toilet soaps undoubtedly took their recipes from natural cosmetics which had gained popularity through common application. The oatmeal face mask, beeswax and lanolin cleansers were all adapted to soaps. Whether their properties remain unchanged after saponification is open to question.

EMOLLIENTS

To make hard tallow soap appropriate as a face cleanser emollients or superfats should be added. Vaseline, lanolin, cold cream and glycerine are all softening agents. When added to soap, they make it easier to lather, and leave a light film on the skin after washing. Fine vegetable oils, such as olive, peanut, palm or safflower should make up twenty per cent of the total volume of fats in a complexion soap. Coconut oil is particularly noted for its quick, abundant, though somewhat thin, lather.

MEDICAMENTS

Besides the toilet and cosmetic soaps, medicated soaps have always been popular. Many of the essential oils used in perfuming soap are highly antiseptic and are therefore also used as preservatives.

In the past, iodine, sulphur, mercurial ointment, benzoic acid, camphor, naphthol were all added to soaps in varying degrees. Mostly they were used to treat skin disorders, both human and animal. Carbolic soap was a favourite, although some controversy arose when it became known that it was highly volatile, losing its antiseptic properties upon exposure to air, rendering it ineffective after one or two washings.

One critic complained that the wrapper had more carbolic odour than the soap bar itself!

Old soap manufacturing manuals from the nineteenth century yield literally hundreds of recipes for every kind of soap. Many cannot be reproduced today due to the scarcity and expense of the natural ingredients. Others, however, can be adapted for the home soaper, producing unique washing aids unavailable on the commercial market. Before experimenting, check the Glossary of Ingredients, Chapter Nine, for a discussion of each additive, its positive effects and possible drawbacks.

7 Pioneer Soap

Cleanliness by the barrelful: the hot, outdoor method

Before commercial dry flaked lye, soap was made by the hot process, using leach from waste ashes. While complete saponification occurs at 185 degrees F with the cold process, the lye-water and fats are actively boiled to produce soap by the hot method.

Although both hard bar soap and soft soap can be made by this method, the latter was the variety most common to the homestead. Made once a year by the barrelful, it was brought up from the cellar in crocks to do general duty as a laundry detergent, floor cleaner, and dishwashing soap. With soft soap, saponification is complete when the mass is thick and creamy. It retains this texture unless the hard soap is extracted by an additional procedure.

For the purist, the pioneer hot process can be reproduced today, although a good soap will require both patience and practice.

A large batch of soft soap is best made outside in a ten-gallon cast-iron pot, such as is used to boil down maple syrup. Melt down twelve pounds of clean rendered beef tallow over a brisk fire. Add lye-water of sufficient strength (see page 43), pouring in slowly. About four five-gallon pails of lye-water will be needed in all. Stir constantly with a "paddle" or broom handle. As the lye works to saponify the fat, the liquid will become stringy and muddy-looking. Continue to add lye-water until the mass is uniformly clear.

If a thick scum of grease forms on top, the lye has been used up and more is needed to saponify the remaining fat. If the soap doesn't thicken and no scum appears, more grease is needed.

To test whether the proper proportions of lye and fat are present, it is necessary to "prove" the soap. As John Carmichael, in his *Treatise on Soapmaking* of 1810 directs, take a clean knife, lift some soap from the kettle and hold it over a plate. If the soap turns whitish and falls from the knife in short pieces, there is too much lye. More grease must be added. If the soap falls from the knife in long ropy pieces, it needs more lye. The soap is suitable when it stands transparent on the knife, neither too white nor too ropy.

Carmichael recommends another way to "prove" soft soap by putting a dollop of soap the size of a pigeon's egg on a glass or china plate. If it cools transparent with whitish streaks and specks, it is done. If the soap is grey and weak-looking or has a grey margin around the outside, it needs more lye. If there is a grey skin over the sample, too much lye is present and more fat must be added.

The traditional homesteader watched the pot to determine when the soap was done. As the soap boils, a froth will rise, a sign that water is evaporating. When the froth no longer rises and the soap seems to settle down in the kettle, it is almost done. Large white bubbles will "pop" over the surface, as if the soap is talking. Remove from heat and cool, then cast into a tight wooden barrel. Because of the caustic nature of this soap, a barrel only lasts a few years before the wood becomes etched by the alkali.

Be careful where the soft soap is set to cool. One farmer recounted this tale from his childhood:

My mother had set a big tub of soap into the barnyard to cool before pouring into the soap barrel. She forgot about it all day. When she went out to milk the cows, she found one of the animals bloated near to bursting. The soap tub was licked clean. The doctor came (there were no veterinarians), made a slit in her side, and the soap came pouring out. The cow lived all right, but we never cooled soap in the barnyard again.

Soft soap can be transformed into hard by further boiling and the addition of salt or rosin. Several handfuls of pickling salt are stirred into the boiling soap, "salting out" the excess water. A red-brown liquid sinks to the bottom and the finished soap rises. As it cools it forms a cake which is removed the next day and boiled with turpentine or rosin and more salt. When thick, it is poured into moulds or shallow pans, cut into bars and hardened.

According to John Carmichael, a pure white hard soap was made commercially without salt or rosin but required repeated boilings. His recipe called for ten hundredweight of the best home melted tallow and two hundred gallons of lye. After several days of two to three boils per day, the soap will pass the "squeeze" test. If a little cooled soap is pinched between the thumb and forefinger, it will squeeze to a thin hard scale. Just before casting into frames, it is coloured and scented.

While such quantities are too cumbersome for the kitchen, the following recipe from the *American Domestic Cyclopaedia of 1890* is not. Two pounds each of melted tallow and sal soda (sodium carbonate) are mixed with one pound of salt and one ounce each of borax, oil of bergamot, and gum camphor. The brew is boiled for an hour, stirring often, and left to cool. It is then warmed again to pouring consistency and cast into moulds.

The development of dry flaked lye has made the cold process method much more reliable than these recipes for the hot process which require a fine eye to test for accurate proportions. The primary function of such homestead soap, however, was not personal washing. More often it found its place in the laundry. Soiled clothes were rubbed with soap, sometimes supplemented with ox gall, a natural detergent. It was not always effective, as one pioneer recalls in *Salt of the Earth*:

Our first venture was getting our clothes washed, of which we had collected a goodly store. The boys drew the water from a hole that had been dug by the side of a slough near the house. It was hard, of that we were in blissful ignorance. What a mess we made of the clothes! The flannels were quite spoiled; the soap stuck to them in little hard lumps and they were sticky and horrid and none of the clothes looked clean. How tired and disheartened we were.

Although the product undoubtedly worked most of the time, its inferior nature, particularly when coupled with hard water, has left this generation with little knowledge of or interest in washing clothes with soap. Two generations of homemakers have been accustomed to synthetic detergents, making any possible switch back to soap fraught with as many misconceptions as grey garments.

The fact that name-brand synthetic detergents are packed inside new automatic washers does not mean that automatics were designed specifically to be used with detergents. In fact, many of the chemicals in detergents are harder on washers than plain, well-made laundry soap (see recipe, page 104). Soap is milder than detergents and cleans just as well under the right conditions.

The biggest problem with soap, if you are not used to it, is what the industry calls soap curd. This is basically the bathtub ring, an insoluble curd that forms when soap reacts with the minerals in hard water. It is difficult to rinse, and if left on your clothes, will eventually leave a tinge of grey.

This problem is overcome by soft water. Either rainwater or spring water can be used, or a mechanical water softener installed. Wash water can also be corrected by adding softeners with each wash. By using a non-phosphate softener, the efficiency of the soap is increased so that less is required. Washing soda, ammonia, or borax can all be used along with soap in amounts which vary with the water hardness.

Be sure to soften the rinse water as well. Otherwise, residual soap remaining in the clothes after spinning will form soap curd.

To discover if your water is hard, try these tests: Does soap lather easily when washing? Are there stains in the toilet and in the drains, which may indicate iron content? When water is boiled in a clean pot, does it leave a white,

dusty deposit? To know for sure, have your water tested or use the method outlined in Chapter Four.

Despite any brainwashing to the contrary, suds are normal with soap, and in fact, desirable. There should always be at least a two-inch head of suds in the washer. If there are no suds, there is not enough soap present to suspend the dirt in the water. Suds are an accurate and important gauge of how well your soap is cleaning. Maintain the suds head all through the wash cycle, checking occasionally to add more soap if necessary.

The amount of soap used will depend on the softness of the water but can be from one to three cups for a full eighteen pound load.

For a really dirty wash, clothes can be presoaked in softened water for a few minutes or overnight. Spot rubbing with a laundry bar will eliminate most stains — even blood.

Soap requires hot water to dissolve properly, but once in a liquid state, it works equally well in lukewarm or cool water. Ideally both wash and rinse water should be lukewarm.

Using soap may require a little more attention in the laundry, but the results are just as good or even superior to detergents. The years of conditioning by detergent manufacturers will gradually wear off: the lemons in the box smell no sweeter than the really "clean" smell of a soap wash. The built-in softeners and stain-removers work no better than a bit of on-the-spot rubbing, and nothing is as soft as a soap wash. Although there is no such thing as whiter than white or brighter than bright, your soap wash can compete favourably with any detergent.

The most important issue in the laundry today is the creation of some balance between clean clothes and a clean environment. Soap, if used properly, can be a solution.

8 Specialty Recipes

"Action is the fruit of knowledge."

— *Fuller*

Before beginning these specialized soap recipes, become familiar with the ingredients, the process and the problems of the test batch of simple soap (Chapter Five). If you have an unsatisfactory result, do another test batch until the soap is successful. Many of the following recipes have more costly ingredients and require more complex procedures, so master the simple formula first.

Read each recipe completely before beginning. This will help avoid misinterpretation. The directions with each recipe are minimal. The method is the same as that outlined in Chapter Five unless specified otherwise. If problems arise, refer to the chart "Soap Defects" on page 67 for possible causes and suggested solutions. Be certain to measure carefully and treat materials with respect.

The fats in all cases should be melted first, then measured, since the recipes were tested with liquid measure. Where vegetable oil is

Basic Soap Chart

FATS	LYE	WATER
1 cup	2 Tbsp.	$^1\!{}_2$ cup
2 cups	¼ cup	$^3\!{}_4$ cup
3 cups	¼ cup+2 Tbsp.	1 cup
4 cups	½ cup	1½ cups
5 cups	½ cup+2 Tbsp.	2 cups
6 cups	¾ cup	$2^1\!{}_4$ cups
7 cups	¾ cup+2 Tbsp.	$2^3\!{}_4$ cups
8 cups	1 cup	3 cups
9 cups	1 cup+2 Tbsp.	3½ cups
10 cups	1¼ cups	$3^3\!{}_4$ cups
11 cups	1¼ cups+2 Tbsp.	4 cups
12 cups	1½ cups	$4^1\!{}_2$ cups
13 cups	1½ cups+2 Tbsp.	5 cups

The following proportions should be remembered when adding or changing ingredients:

Fine vegetable oils:	20% of total fats
Essential oils:	1-2% of total volume
Antiseptic oils:	2-10% of total volume
Fillers:	10-20% of total volume

mentioned, any oil may be used: olive, coconut, palm, peanut, safflower, corn, or just plain salad oil. If you cannot locally purchase any of the ingredients prescribed in the recipes, check Chapter Eleven for the most economical and accessible sources.

Before beginning each recipe, note the yield to determine how many moulds to prepare. When the soap is ready to pour, it will not wait while you find and grease extra moulds.

Although the basic proportion of fat to lye must remain stable, the recipes in other respects are not sacrosanct. For larger batches, increase the ingredients in the proportions indicated in the "Basic Soap Chart" at left. Try experimenting and substituting different kinds of vegetable oils, essential oils, and fillers, using the guidelines indicated in Chapter Six.

Complexion Soaps

Lanolin Soap

Lanolin is a brownish-yellow fatty substance derived from the wool of sheep. Widely used in cosmetics and soap manufacture as a superfatting agent, it produces an extra-rich, creamy cleansing bar which leaves a thin film on your skin, replacing oils lost in washing. Since many people are allergic to lanolin, test for a reaction by rubbing a little on your skin before adding it to the soap. Its slightly unpleasant smell can be masked by a drop of an essential oil such as citronella. Because of the coconut oil content, this soap will require a longer setting and curing time.

1½ cups coconut oil
½ cup clean rendered tallow
2 Tbsp. anhydrous lanolin
1 cup cold soft water
¼ cup lye flakes

1 drop citronella oil (optional)

Prepare moulds by greasing thoroughly with petroleum jelly.

Melt coconut oil and tallow. Measure into ceramic bowl. Stir in lanolin and set aside to cool.

Add lye to cold water, stirring to dissolve. When both mixtures are lukewarm, pour lye solution into fats, stirring constantly. Continue to stir until mass begins to saponify. Add essential oil, if desired. When thick, pour into moulds.

Approximate yield:

3 cups liquid soap
1⅔ lbs. hard bar soap

Vaseline Soap

As a superfatting agent, petrolatum is much less costly, less prone to allergic reaction, and more readily available than lanolin. A fatty jelly-like substance derived from petroleum, it produces a softer soap which leaves a thin, emollient film on the skin.

2 cups clean rendered tallow
½ cup vegetable oil
(2½ cups coconut oil may be substituted for the first two ingredients)

2 Tbsp. Vaseline
1 cup cold soft water
¼ cup plus 1 Tbsp. lye flakes

Melt and measure tallow and vegetable oil. Stir in Vaseline, taking care to thoroughly distribute it. Cool.

Stir lye flakes into cold water until completely dissolved. Set aside to cool.

Grease moulds liberally with petroleum jelly.

When lye and fat are lukewarm, pour lye into fat slowly, stirring constantly. Continue to stir until the mixture becomes thick and creamy. Pour into moulds.

Approximate yield:

3⅔ cups liquid soap
1¾ lbs. hard bar soap

Borax Soap

Borax is a white crystalline compound used as an antiseptic, preservative, and cleanser, as well as water softener. Found naturally in the western United States, it produces a very white, extra mild soap for delicate skin.

4 cups coconut oil
1 cup clean rendered tallow
2 cups cold soft water

½ cup lye flakes
⅓ cup borax
½ cup boiling water

Dissolve borax in boiling water.

Melt coconut oil and tallow. Set aside to cool. Stir lye flakes into cold water until completely dissolved. Set aside to cool.

Grease moulds liberally with petroleum jelly.

When lye and fat are lukewarm, pour lye slowly into fat, stirring constantly. Continue to stir until the mixture becomes thick and creamy. Add the borax solution and continue to stir until the mixture is thick. Pour into moulds.

Approximate yield:
7½ cups liquid soap
3¾ lbs. hard bar soap

Camomile Soap

Camomile is an herb valued as much for external use as internal. This small yellow-centred flower with white rays was consecrated by the Egyptians to their gods. Long one of nature's cosmetics, it is said that brushing the face with soap and camomile will keep the skin smooth, supple, and young. In the mid-1800s, a soap made with the flowers of this "physician's plant" was a popular addition to the children's bath. It passed out of fashion toward the turn of the century, but was still included in a list of recipes from 1898. Originally tinted blue with ultramarine, it also called for a blend of lavender, bergamot, caraway, and rosemary oils.

1 cup clean rendered tallow	2 Tbsp. camomile flowers
½ cup coconut oil	¼ cup talc or fuller's earth (optional)
½ cup olive oil	
1 cup cold soft water	a few grains of powdered laundry blueing (optional)
¼ cup lye flakes	

Using a mortar and pestle, grind the dried flowers to a fine powder. Mix with talc or fuller's earth, then add olive oil gradually, stirring to dissolve. (Alternatively, heat the flowers in the olive oil, simmering for a half hour. Strain and gradually add to talc or fuller's earth.)

Melt tallow and coconut oil. Set aside to cool. Stir lye flakes into cold water until completely dissolved. Cool.

Grease moulds with petroleum jelly.

When fats and lye water are lukewarm, add lye to fat stirring constantly. Stir until mixture thickens to the consistency of creamed honey. Add the camomile-olive oil mixture and colorant, stirring well to distribute evenly. Pour into moulds.

Approximate yield:
3 cups liquid soap
1⅔ lbs. hard bar soap

Yolk Soap

Egg yolk is a common ingredient in cosmetics and hair preparations, but egg yolk soap is no longer available commercially. In a soapmaster's book from 1881 this simple recipe for yolk soap was claimed to be beneficial to the skin. Although it has been scaled down to household proportions, the recipe is unchanged except for the addition of wheat germ oil or vitamin E oil as anti-oxidants and the optional essential oils.

2 cups clean rendered tallow	1 tsp. wheat germ oil or vitamin E oil (external use)
2 cups coconut oil	1 tsp. oil of lemon (optional)
5 egg yolks and enough olive oil to make one cup	½ tsp. oil of sassafras (optional)
2 cups cold soft water	¼ tsp. each oil of cloves and thyme (optional)
½ cup plus 2 Tbsp. lye flakes	

Beat egg yolks till pale, adding olive oil to measure one cup.

Melt tallow and coconut oil. Set aside to cool.

Stir lye into cold water until dissolved. Set aside to cool.

Grease moulds liberally with petroleum jelly.

When lye and fat are lukewarm, stir lye slowly into fat. Continue to stir until the mixture begins to thicken. Add egg mixture and beat to distribute evenly. Add essential oils, if desired. Continue to stir until thick and creamy. Pour into moulds.

This soap will require longer setting and curing times.

Approximate yield:
7 cups liquid soap
3½ lbs. hard bar soap

Pine Soap

A very lightly scented pine soap can derive its perfume from the needles of coniferous trees. In the winter, when fragrant blossoms are only a memory, these evergreens provide a pleasantly aromatic soap.

2 cups pine needles, freshly gathered	½ cup vegetable oil
1 cup water	¼ cup cold soft water
1½ cups clean rendered tallow	¼ cup lye flakes

Cut needles into pieces and boil five minutes in one cup water. Steep ten minutes and strain. You should have pine-scented water.

Melt tallow and vegetable oil. Set aside to cool. Add lye to water, stirring to dissolve. Cool.

Grease moulds liberally with petroleum jelly.

When fat and lye are lukewarm, pour lye into fat, stirring constantly. When beginning to thicken, add pine water and stir until thick and creamy. Pour into moulds.

Approximate yield:

2¾ cups liquid soap

1½ lbs. hard bar soap

Windsor Soap

Windsor soap was a stock item of almost every soaper in the nineteenth century. At the Great Exhibition of 1851 in London, England, where there were 727 exhibitors in the soap and perfumery section, Yardley and Statham won an award for a cake of Brown Windsor soap. This same bar was again exhibited a hundred years later, still in prime condition, at the Victoria & Albert Centenary Exhibition. This spicy brown soap has many recipe variations, but the primary component is always oil of caraway. Since this scent is somewhat fleeting, it is usually blended with the more stable oils of sassafras, cloves and bergamot.

7 cups clean rendered tallow	1 tsp. oil of cinnamon
2 cups vegetable oil	¼ tsp. each oil of cloves and caraway
3½ cups cold soft water	½ tsp. each oil of sassafras and bergamot
1 cup plus 2 Tbsp. lye flakes	

Measure and blend essential oils.

Melt tallow and vegetable oil. Set aside to cool. Stir lye flakes into cold water until dissolved and set aside to cool.

Grease moulds liberally with petroleum jelly.

When lye and fat are lukewarm, stir lye slowly into fat, until mixture is thick and creamy.

Add essential oils, beating well to disperse evenly. Pour into moulds.

Approximate yield:
13 cups liquid soap
6 lbs. hard bar soap

Note: a mock Windsor soap can be made by simmering one-half cup chopped caraway seeds in tallow, to be used in a standard soap recipe. Strain out seeds, then tint with cinnamon.

Honey Soap

Although virtually every soapmaster's book contained a recipe for honey soap, nowhere was honey mentioned as an ingredient. Generally it was simply a plain white toilet soap flavoured with citronella and various combinations of the oils of lemon grass, cassia, thyme and caraway. The addition of beeswax to the recipe below imparts a faint sweet aroma as well as giving some meaning to the soap's name. Honey may be added, which gives the soap an amber colour, and softer texture.

1½ cups clean rendered tallow
½ cup vegetable oil
3 Tbsp. pure beeswax
¾ cup cold soft water
¼ cup lye flakes
1 tsp. citronella oil
¼ tsp. oil of lemon grass (optional)
2 Tbsp. liquid honey (optional)

Melt beeswax in a double boiler over hot water till liquid. Beat in vegetable oil and keep warm. Melt tallow and measure. Stir lye flakes into cold water until dissolved. Set aside to cool.

Grease moulds liberally with petroleum jelly.

When lye and tallow are lukewarm, pour lye slowly into fat, stirring until thick and creamy.

Add warm wax mixture in a thin stream, beating vigorously to disperse evenly. Add honey and essential oils. Pour into moulds.

Approximate yield:
2¾ cups liquid soap
1½ lbs. hard bar soap

Blossom Bars

The delicate scent of a spring blossom cannot

be duplicated synthetically. Even the essential oil distilled from a flower will lose that subtle freshness. Lock some of the sweetness into your soap and enjoy the fragrance all year long.

4 packed cups blossoms (apple, cherry, rose)	2 cups cold soft water
4 cups rendered tallow	½ cup plus 2 Tbsp. lye flakes
1 cup vegetable oil (approximately)	

Gather fresh, strong-scented blossoms early in the morning and immerse in melted tallow. Heat very gently for an hour. Keep just at melting point, if possible. Allow to harden overnight, then remelt gently and strain.

Add vegetable oil to blossom tallow to make 5 cups and set aside to cool. Stir lye flakes into cold water until dissolved and set aside to cool.

Grease moulds liberally with petroleum jelly.

When lye and fat are lukewarm, pour lye slowly into fat, stirring to emulsify. Continue to stir until thick. Pour into moulds.

Approximate yield:
7 cups liquid soap
3½ lbs. hard bar soap

Cinnamon Soap

This creamy chocolate-coloured soap smells distinctly of cinnamon. The spicy grains result in a lightly abrasive bar, which becomes more pronounced if more cinnamon is added. For a lighter soap, use less spice.

1½ cups clean rendered tallow	¼ cup lye flakes
½ cup vegetable oil	1 Tbsp. powdered cinnamon
¾ cup cold soft water	

Measure 1 tablespoon of the vegetable oil and add to the cinnamon, mixing thoroughly.

Melt tallow and remaining vegetable oil. Cool in a large ceramic bowl. Add lye to cold water, stirring until dissolved. Set aside to cool.

Grease moulds thoroughly with petroleum jelly.

When fat and lye are lukewarm, pour the lye solution slowly into the fat, stirring constantly. Continue to stir until the mixture has saponified.

When the soap is thick, just before pouring into moulds, add the cinnamon-oil mixture, beating until thoroughly combined. Pour into moulds.

Approximate yield:

2¾ cups liquid soap

1½ lbs. hard bar soap

Salmon Soap

There is nothing fishy about this soap except the colour. The red spice produces a lovely lightly-speckled salmon shade, otherwise virtually impossible to achieve by any means other than synthetic dye. Despite the peppery additive, this soap is not at all harsh.

1½ cups clean rendered tallow	¾ cup cold soft water
	¼ cup lye flakes
½ cup vegetable oil	1 Tbsp. powdered paprika

Measure 2 tablespoons of the vegetable oil. Add to paprika and stir until thoroughly mixed.

Melt tallow and remaining vegetable oil. Cool in a large ceramic bowl. Add lye to cold water, stirring until completely dissolved and set aside to cool.

Grease moulds thoroughly with petroleum jelly.

When fat and lye have cooled to room temperature, pour the lye solution slowly into the fat stirring constantly.

Continue to stir until the mixture is as thick as honey, then add the paprika mixture, beating vigorously until evenly distributed. Pour into moulds.

Approximate yield:

3 cups liquid soap

1½ lbs. hard bar soap

Anise Soap

In the sixteenth century, anise was widely

used as mousetrap bait. The sweet licorice aroma of this herb is equally irresistible to humans. Soapmasters of 150 years ago relied on anise and caraway as the primary sources for the essential oils used in soap.

¼ cup anise seeds	¼ cup vegetable oil
¼ cup lard or tallow	½ cup cold soft water
¾ cup tallow (approx.)	2 Tbsp. lye

Heat the ¼ cup of tallow or lard until melted. Add anise seed and simmer over lowest heat for half an hour. If you have a wood stove, set on back all day. Leave to solidify for a few hours or overnight, then melt again and strain seeds.

Add enough additional melted tallow to the strained anise fat to measure ¾ cup. Add vegetable oil and set aside to cool.

Stir lye into cold water until thoroughly dissolved and set aside to cool.

Grease moulds liberally with petroleum jelly.

When lye and fat are lukewarm, pour lye into fat, stirring constantly. Continue to stir until the mixture has saponified and is as thick as creamed honey. Pour into moulds.

Approximate yield:

1½ cups liquid soap

12 oz. hard bar soap

Lettuce or Cucumber Soap

Two of the more exotic soaps on early soapers' shelves, cucumber and lettuce, were purported to have curative properties. Cucumber juice has long been used as an astringent facewash. The original recipe for this toilet bar includes ingredients difficult for the home soapmaker to procure, such as cassia pomade, spermaceti, and oil of valerian. Hence, a modified version is offered here.

1½ cups clean rendered tallow	¼ cup lye flakes
1 cup cucumber pulp or chopped lettuce	½ tsp. wheat germ oil or vitamin E oil (external use)
½ cup vegetable oil	
¾ cup cold soft water	2 drops oil of cloves (optional)

Grate cucumber fine, peel and all, or chop lettuce fine. Melt tallow and add lettuce or cucumber. Keep on lowest heat for half an hour or on back of wood stove for several hours. The fat may then be strained or used as is. The pulp will add tiny greenish-yellow specks to the soap.

Add vegetable oil to fat and set aside to cool. Stir lye flakes into cold water until dissolved and set aside to cool.

Grease moulds thoroughly with petroleum jelly.

When fat and lye are lukewarm, add lye to fat slowly, stirring constantly. Continue to stir until the mixture is thick and creamy. Add wheat germ oil or vitamin E oil, and a drop or two of oil of cloves, beating well to distribute evenly.

Pour into moulds.
Approximate yield:
2¾ cups liquid soap
1½ lbs. hard bar soap

Vegetarian Soap

Strict vegetarians have limited options in cleaning products since most use at least some animal fats. The following recipe will produce a toilet soap made entirely of vegetable oils. The suggestions for colouring, fragrances and fillers can all be adapted to this basic bar. When well-cured, this soap has a copious though somewhat thin lather. Since coconut oil is not very sensitive to electrolytes such as salt, it will lather in seawater, making it a good marine soap. It is softer than tallow soap and may not be as long-lasting nor as economical to use.

2 cups coconut oil or 100 per cent solid vegetable shortening	¾ cup cold soft water
	¼ cup lye flakes

Melt coconut oil until liquid but not too warm. It has a very low melting point, so don't heat unnecessarily.

Add lye to cold water, stirring to dissolve.
Grease moulds liberally with petroleum jelly.

96

When lye and fat are cooled, pour lye into fat, stirring constantly. This recipe takes a long time to saponify — up to an hour. It is not necessary to stir for the entire time, but do keep it well-mixed as it thickens.

When thick, pour into moulds. It sets very slowly. After a day it will be firm but may not be hard enough to use for several weeks.
Approximate yield:
2¾ cups liquid soap
1½ lbs. hard bar soap

Glass Soap

Transparent soaps have a special appeal, their clarity associated with purity. Any good quality homemade soap can be made transparent since it is essentially a conversion from the crystalline to the colloidal state. The basic method involves dissolving soap shavings in an equal amount of alcohol over very low heat. The mixture is then simmered gently to distil off 80 per cent of the alcohol before pouring in-

to moulds. Since glycerine promotes transparency, the following recipe will produce a high quality soap the colour of amber glass.
Note: Do not double recipe since the process is difficult to control in large quantities.

1 cup tallow	¾ cup water
⅓ cup melted coconut oil	4 Tbsp. lye flakes
⅔ cups glycerine	yellow food colouring
1-1½ cups isopropyl alcohol (70 per cent)	

Melt tallow and coconut oil. Set aside to cool. Stir lye flakes into cold soft water until dissolved, then cool.

Grease moulds liberally with petroleum jelly. (Moulds must have a tight seal since the soap is very hot and liquid when poured.)

When lye and fat are lukewarm, pour lye into fat, stirring to emulsify. Continue to stir until thick and creamy. Add glycerine. Pour into mould. When set hard (three days) grate into a shallow pot. (There should be about three cups of grated soap.) Be sure the soap is grated finely and evenly since larger pieces will take longer to melt. Add alcohol to the soap and stir to moisten. Add colouring. Set the pot in a larger pan of gently boiling water. (Do not let the water boil over into the soap.) Stir constantly as the alcohol heats and the soap granules dissolve. Alcohol has a very low boiling point, so will quickly begin to evaporate. Continue to stir until the liquid is transparent. Frequently lift the spoon from the liquid. When a ropy thread forms, the soap is almost ready. Remove the pot from the heat a moment. If a thin skin forms on top, pour immediately into greased moulds. If not, return to heat and watch closely until liquid threads from spoon. Pour into moulds. When hard, the soap will be clear amber with a quick, gentle lather.

Approximate yield:
3 cups liquid soap
1½ lbs. hard bar soap

Cleansing Creams

Even simple soap without additives is harsh for some complexions which react to the smallest amount of alkali. A cleansing cream, however, is actually a non-alkaline emollient which is spread lightly, then wiped off the skin, taking with it dirt, debris and sebum (secretion from the skin's oil glands). Following the cleansing cream, use an astringent (i.e. equal parts of witch hazel and water, or vinegar and water, or fresh mashed strawberry puree), to dissolve any oily, waxy residue.

Coconut Cleanser

3 Tbsp. coconut oil	1 Tbsp. glycerine
1 Tbsp. olive oil	2 tsp. water

Melt ingredients together over very low heat until liquid. Remove from heat. Beat as the mixture cools to emulsify. Store in an airtight jar and keep in the refrigerator since coconut oil has a very low melting point.

Olive Cream

½ tsp. borax   4 Tbsp. Vaseline
2 tsp. boiling water 4 Tbsp. olive oil

Dissolve borax in boiling water. Melt Vaseline and olive oil over low heat till liquid. Add borax-water. Stir to mix thoroughly. Remove from heat. Beat as the mixture cools, to emulsify. Store in the refrigerator.

Medicated Soaps

Camphor Ice Soap

The medicine chest of a century ago was stocked not with chemical sprays and foams but often held, among the salves and ointments, a variety of special-purpose soaps. Camphorated soap was considered essential, used to clean cuts and scratches and treat skin conditions. Although its smell is reminiscent of chest colds and pulled muscles, its topical anaesthetic quality produces a pleasant cooling effect.

1½ cups clean rendered   ¾ cup cold soft water
tallow   ¼ cup lye flakes
½ cup coconut oil   2 tsp. camphorated oil

Melt tallow and coconut oil. Set aside to cool. Stir lye flakes into water until completely dissolved. Set aside to cool.

Grease moulds liberally with petroleum jelly.

When lye and fat are lukewarm, pour lye slowly into fat, stirring constantly. Continue to stir until mixture becomes thick and creamy. Just before pouring into moulds, add camphorated oil, beating to disperse thoroughly. Pour into moulds.

Approximate yield:

2¾ cups liquid soap
1½ lbs. hard bar soap

Carbolic Soap

Many people of this generation still have memories, fond and otherwise, of the pungent odour of carbolic soap. A disinfectant, it was the stand-by of rural back-kitchens, used to remove "the smell of the barn." Around the turn of the century, dog soap was made by adding five per cent carbolic acid to rancid soap stock, and colouring it with caramel. A poisonous, powerful antiseptic, it is also very volatile, losing its effect on long exposure to air. It is best to make this soap in small batches, as you need it. To store, wrap well in heavy waxed paper or plastic wrap.

¾ cup clean rendered tallow	1 tsp. carbolic acid (liquified phenol B.P.)
¼ cup vegetable oil	1 drop oil of cloves (optional)
½ cup cold soft water	
2 Tbsp. lye flakes	2 drops oil of lavender (optional)

Melt vegetable oil and tallow. Set aside to cool. Stir lye flakes into cold water until completely dissolved. Set aside to cool.

Grease moulds liberally with petroleum jelly.

When fat and lye are lukewarm, stir lye slowly into fat. Continue to stir until the mixture becomes thick and creamy.

Add carbolic acid, stirring vigorously to distribute evenly. Pour into moulds.

Approximate yield:

1½ cups liquid soap

12 oz. hard bar soap

Sulphur Soap

Another medicated soap, sulphur was added to soothe skin disorders. This pale yellow, non-metallic crystalline element was purported to be effective for everything from ringworm to washing the dog.

¾ cup clean rendered tallow	2 Tbsp. lye flakes
¼ cup vegetable oil	1½ Tbsp. flowers of sulphur
½ cup cold soft water	

Add one tablespoon of the vegetable oil to the sulphur, stirring to a paste.

Melt tallow and remaining vegetable oil. Set aside to cool. Stir lye flakes into cold water until dissolved and set aside to cool.

Grease moulds liberally with petroleum jelly.

When lye and fat are lukewarm, pour lye slowly into fat, stirring constantly. Continue to stir until mixture becomes thick and creamy. Add sulphur and beat to disperse evenly. Pour into moulds.

Approximate yield:

1½ cups liquid soap

12 oz. hard bar soap

Filled Soaps

Pumice Paste Hand Soap

This soap, if kept well sealed, will remain soft indefinitely. With the addition of sand or pumice it makes a terrific hand cleaner after greasy, dirty work. Use clean, washed sand or coarse pumice from a construction supplier. Any good quality soap, even laundry bars, can be used as the base.

1 lb. hard soap, grated   2 cups water

4 Tbsp. mineral oil or   1 lb. clean sand or pumice
baby oil

Shave or grate well-cured soap into the top of a double boiler. Be careful not to use aluminum or tin graters as they will become discoloured. Add water and heat very slowly. Do not rush the heating process or you will end up with an unmanageable mess. If heated properly, the soap will turn transparent, then liquefy. Stir while melting to mix soap and water thoroughly.

When melted, remove from heat and mix in mineral oil or baby oil. Stir in sand or pumice until evenly distributed. It will be a very stiff dough.

When thoroughly mixed, store in jars with tight-fitting lids.

Approximate yield:

5 cups soap paste

Sand Soap

Nothing cleans really tough dirt, ground into

the pores, like sand soap. Before soap was commonly available, the pioneer housewife used sand and lye-water for much of her household cleaning. This soap works wonders on greasy dirt and deep stains, as well as on hard-earned callouses.

1½ cups clean rendered tallow	¼ cup lye flakes
½ cup vegetable oil	½ cup fine washed sand or coarse pumice
1 cup cold soft water	

Add the vegetable oil to sand or pumice, stirring well.

Melt tallow and set aside to cool. Add lye flakes to cold water, stirring to dissolve. Set aside to cool.

Grease moulds liberally with petroleum jelly.

When lye and fat are lukewarm, pour lye into fat, stirring constantly. When saponified to a creamy stage, add sand-oil mixture slowly, stirring well. Combine thoroughly and evenly, then pour into moulds.

Approximate yield:

3½ cups liquid soap
1¾ lbs. hard bar soap

Abrasive Complexion Soap.

A variety of milled grains were once added to soaps to enhance their cosmetic value. Long before soap was in regular use, the skin was stimulated and cleansed with a mixture of rainwater and milled grain. Cornmeal is the harshest of the three, and adds a tinge of yellow to the soap. Oatmeal and bran produce a beige speckled bar, with bran being the least abrasive. Traditional oatmeal bars used oat groats and were often lightly perfumed with oils of sassafras, cassia and lavender. The quantity of abrasive filler may vary from 10 to 20 per cent of the total volume.

1½ cups clean rendered tallow	¼ cup lye flakes
½ cup coconut oil	½ cup lightly toasted bran, oatmeal, or cornmeal
¾ cup cold soft water	¼ tsp. oil of cassia, sassafras or lavender (optional)
½ tsp. wheat germ oil or vitamin E oil (external use)	

Melt coconut oil and tallow, set aside to cool. Stir lye flakes into cold water until completely dissolved.

Grease moulds well with petroleum jelly.

When lye and fat are lukewarm, add the lye slowly to the fat, stirring constantly. Continue to stir until the mixture begins to thicken. Add grain gradually, beating until it is distributed evenly throughout the saponified mass. The thickening process will be accelerated by the filler, so don't delay before adding it. Pour into moulds.

Approximate yield:

3 cups liquid soap
1⅔ lbs. hard bar soap

Fuller's Earth Soap

Fuller's earth is a fine, chalk-like substance used as a dusting powder for babies with sensitive skin and as a fabric grease-stain remover. It was so named because it was originally used to remove lanolin in the fulling (cleaning) of woolen cloth. Before the turn of the century, most soap manufacturers offered a baby soap containing fuller's earth. This absorbent mixture of silica and clay produces a greyish, lacklustre bar which has the softest silkiest lather. Its grease-absorbent properties make it effective for oily skin.

¾ cup clean rendered tallow	½ cup cold soft water
	2 Tbsp. lye flakes
¼ cup vegetable oil	¼ cup fuller's earth

Add vegetable oil gradually to fuller's earth, mixing to a smooth paste. Grease moulds with petroleum jelly.

Melt tallow, then set aside to cool. Add lye to water, stirring constantly until dissolved. When lye and fat have cooled to lukewarm, add lye to fat slowly, stirring constantly.

When the mixture begins to thicken, add fuller's earth mixture. Stir well to distribute evenly, as it will thicken quickly. Pour into moulds. Approximate yield:

1½ cups liquid soap
12 oz. hard bar soap

Special Purpose Soaps

Bug Soap

Commercial fragrant soaps often attract annoying biting insects during the warm summer months. There are some odours, such as lavender, eucalyptus and citronella, which are pleasant to people yet repulsive to bugs. Although using such additives will not eliminate the problem, they will make you less appetizing to arthropods.

1½ cups clean rendered tallow	1 Tbsp. citronella oil or
½ cup coconut oil	1 Tbsp. eucalyptus oil or
¾ cup cold soft water	
¼ cup lye flakes	1 Tbsp. lavender oil

Melt tallow and vegetable oil. Set aside to cool. Stir lye into cold water until dissolved and set aside to cool.

Grease moulds liberally with petroleum jelly.

When lye and fat are lukewarm, pour lye into fat slowly, stirring constantly. When mixture becomes thick and creamy, add essential oil, beating vigorously to distribute evenly throughout. Pour into moulds.
Approximate yield:
2¾ cups liquid soap
1½ lbs. hard bar soap

Glycerine & Herbal Shampoo

A pleasant-smelling, lathering shampoo can be made as easily as soap. The base for this gentle hair cleanser is, in fact, the Glass Soap recipe found on page 96. Prepare the soap recipe as directed but do not proceed to the alcohol phase. When the fat-lye mixture has thickened, pour all but 1 cup into moulds. To this reserved soap add 1 cup of warm soft water and ¼ cup melted coconut oil. One-quarter cup of baby shampoo may be added for extra lather. Beat together thoroughly until smooth and creamy white. As it sets, stir occasionally. It will require about an hour to reach the consistency of cold cream. When set, seal tightly in jars. This recipe makes about 20 ounces of shampoo.

For those with oily hair, a superior cleanser is produced by adding 3 tablespoons of baking soda dissolved in 2 teaspoons of water to the above mixture.

Fragrant herbal shampoos can be made by replacing the water with herbal teas. Add 2 tablespoons of strongly scented herbs to a cup of water and boil gently 15 minutes. Pour into a glass container, cool, and let stand overnight. Strain, then add water to measure 1 cup and use.

Best Laundry Soap

Soap cleans clothes just as well as detergents. A heretical statement in this day, it is nevertheless true, provided proper procedures are followed. For a detailed description of washing clothes with soap, see pages 81-83.

8 cups clean rendered tallow	2½ Tbsp. borax
1 cup lye flakes	1 tsp. table salt
2 cups cold soft water	1 cup boiling water

Melt tallow, measure and set aside to cool. Stir lye flakes into cold water until thoroughly dissolved. Cool.

Dissolve borax and salt in boiling water.

Grease large mould liberally with petroleum jelly.

When tallow and lye are cooled to lukewarm, pour lye slowly into fat, stirring constantly. Continue to stir until mixture thickens. Add borax and salt solution, and stir until thick.

Pour into mould. After an hour or two, when soap is the consistency of cold butter, cut with a knife into large bars.

Once set, remove from mould and stack brick-like for at least two weeks to cure. To use, shave or grate into hot water. When dissolved, add to softened wash water and agitate lightly before adding soiled clothes.

Approximate yield:
5 lbs. hard bar soap (20 cups, grated)

Insect Soap Spray

Pear slugs and other fruit pests can be destroyed by frequent applications of the following mixture, according to the 1873 edition of *Canada Farmer*. Soap was often used in home insect remedies as an emulsifier, to maintain the other ingredients in suspension. The soap solution itself is not harmful to plants. In fact, before the days of indoor plumbing and synthetic detergents, many housewives tossed the dishwater on the rose bed to keep insects from the precious buds.

12 gal. cold water	1 lb. hard laundry soap
1 bushel ashes	dissolved in hot water
½ peck unslaked lime	

Add ashes and lime to cold water and allow to settle 24 hours. Add soft soap and mix thoroughly. Spray with a garden syringe on affected plants.

An oil spray using soap as an emulsifier can also be used to suffocate early spring insects, particularly on fruit trees. Apply while the trees are still in a dormant leafless state, covering the tree thoroughly with each spraying.

1 gal. light-grade oil	½ gal. warm water
1 lb. hard laundry soap	

Dissolve soap in water. Add oil and mix well to emulsify. Dilute with 20 times more water before use.

Leather Soap

Leather should be cleaned occasionally before applying preserving oils. Using a wet sponge, rub some of this soap into leather and dry with a clean cloth. When the leather has thus been cleaned and dried, preserve it by rubbing in a warm mixture of equal parts neat's-foot oil and mineral oil. To waterproof leather, rub with a mixture of 1½ oz. mineral oil, 1 oz. tallow, and 5 oz. neat's-foot oil. Do not use on suede.

1½ cups clean rendered tallow	½ cup melted beeswax
¼ cup neat's-foot oil (or compound)	¾ cup cold soft water
	¼ cup lye flakes

Stir lye flakes into cold water until dissolved. Melt 1 cup tallow. Add neat's-foot oil and set aside to cool.

Melt beeswax in the top of a double boiler. Add remaining ½ cup tallow to beeswax, stirring to melt and mix thoroughly. Retain tallow-wax mixture in hot water to liquefy.

Grease moulds thoroughly with petroleum jelly.

When fat and lye are lukewarm, pour lye slowly into fat, stirring constantly to emulsify. Beating vigorously, add tallow-wax mixture in a thin stream. The wax will cool and solidify quickly. Continue to beat till thick. Pour immediately into moulds.

Approximate yield:
2¾ cups liquid soap
1½ lbs. hard bar soap

Shaving Soap

Although electric razors have replaced the strap and blade in many bathrooms, there are those who still prefer the ritual of lather and brush. Ideally, a shaving soap should be neutral to prevent irritation, produce a copious, creamy lather, soften the skin to prevent cuts, and be antiseptic to clean and soothe the inevitable nicks. All of these demands require a wide variety of ingredients, but the result is well worth the extra effort and expense.

½ cup clean rendered tallow	2 Tbsp. lye flakes
¼ cup coconut oil	½ tsp. eucalyptus oil
2 Tbsp. glycerine	½ tsp. camphorated oil
2 Tbsp. lanolin	¼ tsp. each oil of cloves and cinnamon (or powdered)
1½ tsp. melted beeswax	
½ cup cold soft water	2 tsp. fuller's earth

As moulds, use shaving mug and rounds

which will fit into the mug (cardboard frozen orange juice containers). Grease these rounds with petroleum jelly.

Melt together tallow, coconut oil and beeswax. Set aside to cool. Stir lye flakes into cold water until dissolved, then cool.

When fat and lye are lukewarm, pour lye slowly into fat, stirring to thicken. Add lanolin, glycerine and essential oils, beating vigorously to disperse evenly. Pour into mug and greased rounds.

Approximate yield:
1½ cups liquid soap
12 oz. hard bar soap

Toothpaste

Commercial toothpastes are a complex combination of ingredients. Basically a medïum, or paste, suspends a small amount of fine pumice which abrades stains. The foaming action of the paste carries off particles loosened by brushing. The flavourings, preservatives and colourings serve no useful function in cleaning the teeth or mouth. In fact, many dentists agree that the action of proper brushing itself, even without paste, effectively dislodges food particles and thus freshens the mouth. In the days before the tube, teeth were cleaned with baking soda or salt, both effective abrasives. Following is a recipe for a toothpaste which is more pleasant tasting than either of the above, and just as effective as the commercial products. If a homemade paste is used regularly, check with your dentist for information on alternate sources of fluoride.

8 Tbsp. baking soda	1-2 tsp. flavouring (e.g.
3 Tbsp. glycerine	peppermint, wintergreen)

Blend ingredients thoroughly and store in a well-sealed glass container. To use, dip moistened brush in the paste.

Approximate yield: ⅓ cup

9 Glossary of Ingredients

"Man does not live by soap alone; and hygiene is not much good unless you take a healthy view of it...."

— *G.K. Chesterton*

Following is a list of the materials contained in the recipes outlined in this book and some of those common to commercial cosmetic preparations. An attempt has been made to define each ingredient, as well as to indicate its uses and effects, both positive and negative. See Chapter Ten for clarification. The most likely source for each item is indicated after each description.

Alcohol (Isopropyl)
Petroleum by-product available in varying strengths. Solvent, astringent, antiseptic. May dry skin and hair. (Pharmacy)

Alum
Colourless, odourless, crystalline powder. Derives from natural sources including soils and minerals such as bauxite, cryolite, alum stone. Used in production of medicines, sugar, textiles, deodorants. Astringent. Possible contact dermatitis, skin irritations. (Pharmacy, Grocery)

Ammonia (NH$_3$)

Occurs naturally in air, water, animal elimination. Colourless, alkaline gas, a by-product of some industries. Dissolved in water it is known as spirits of hartshorn or aqua ammonia. Used as fertilizer, in explosives, synthetic dye. Household ammonia is a dilute solution of ammonium hydroxide. Do not breathe vapours; avoid skin contact. Alkali. (Pharmacy)

Anise (Pimpinella anisum)

Cultivated world-wide for its seedlike fruit which is used to produce a fragrant oil for cooking and cosmetics. Applied directly to skin can cause redness, scaling. Irritant. (Pharmacy, Natural Food Store, Grocery)

Balsam

A resin which contains benzoic acid and/or cinnamic acid. Balsam of Peru from an Asian tree is used in perfumery but has no medicinal value. Liquid storax has pleasant odour, used in medicine as external application in some parasitic skin diseases. Canada Balsam (balsam of fir) is a turpentine, not a true balsam. (Pharmacy, Essential Oil Supplier)

Beeswax

A highly fragrant natural animal wax, from the honeycomb of beehive frames. Soluble in oils. Melting point 143-149 degrees F. Emulsifier, base in cosmetics. (Craft Store, Apiary)

Benzoic Acid

Nontoxic, aromatic compound separated by heat from benzoin, a tropical gum resin. White scales or needle-like crystals soluble in alcohol. Antiseptic, preservative, fungicide. Retards rancidity and darkening. Used widely in margarine, cosmetics, skin salves and soaps. Possible allergic skin rashes. (Pharmacy)

Bergamot Oil *(Citrus bergamia)*
Honey-coloured oil from the rind of a lemon-shaped fruit of the bergamot tree, a member of the rue family. Aromatic. Possible eczema. Potential photosensitizer. (Essential Oil Supplier)

Borax $(Na_2B_4O_7)$
Crystalline compound found naturally in salt deposits of western U.S. White alkaline powder, moderately soluble in water. Used as antiseptic, preservative, cleanser, flux, soap supplement, water softener. (Pharmacy, Pottery Supply House)

Camomile *(Matricaria chamomilla)*
Flowers of this strong-scented member of the aster family have long been used as a tonic. Oil distilled from the plant sometimes used medicinally and in perfumes and shampoos. Anti-irritant, demulcent, natural colorant. (Natural Food Store)

Camphor *(Cinnamomum camphora)* $(C_{10}H_{16}O)$
Aromatic, white waxy substance obtained from camphor laurel, Asiatic evergreen, reduced to colourless or white crystals by steam distillation. Dissolved in alcohol, known as spirits of camphor. Astringent, antiseptic, topical anaesthetic and preservative. Posssible allergic skin rashes. Vapours flammable. (Pharmacy)

Caraway *(Carum carvi)*
Fruit of member of carrot family widely cultivated in Europe and America. Yields aromatic, spicy volatile oil. Used in medicine and flavouring. (Natural Food Store, Grocery)

Carbolic Acid
Caustic poison derived from carbon and oil. Antiseptic, disinfectant. Possible photosensitizer. (Pharmacy)

Castor Oil
Fixed oil obtained by pressing castor bean

seeds. Becomes hard, wax-like fat by hydrogenation. Emollient. Used in cosmetics, hair oils, formerly in soaps. (Pharmacy)

Caustic Potash (Potassium hydroxide)

White flakes soluble in alcohol, water or glycerine. Made by electrolysis of a potassium chloride solution. Caution: Highly toxic by ingestion, skin irritant. (Pharmacy)

Caustic Soda (Sodium hydroxide)

Commonly purchased lye flakes. White chips soluble in water or alcohol. Made by electrolysis of a sodium chloride solution. Heats on contact with water, can cause severe burns to skin. Handle with care. Store in airtight containers. (Pharmacy, Grocery, Hardware)

Cinnamon

Aromatic inner bark of tropical laurel. Coarse variety of cinnamon known as cassia. Used as flavouring. (Grocery, Natural Food Store)

Citronella Oil

Aromatic light-yellow essential oil, soluble in alcohol. Derived by steam distillation of the grass of *Cymbopogon nardus*. May cause stuffy or runny nose, asthma, contact dermatitis. Toxic if taken internally. (Natural Food Store, Essential Oil Supplier)

Clove Oil

Essential oil extracted from the tropical evergreen tree of the myrtle family. Aromatic, antiseptic. Can cause contact dermatitis, allergic reactions. (Natural Food Store, Essential Oil Supplier)

Cocoa Butter

Pure fat extracted by pressure from ground and crushed cocoa bean. Used in cooking, cosmetics, medicinally to treat skin irritations. Emollient. May cause allergic reactions in those sensitized to chocolate. (Pharmacy, Natural Food Store)

Coconut Oil
One thousand mature nuts yield 25 gal. oil, solid at room temperature. Soluble in alcohol. Melting point 83 degrees F. Cleanser, emollient. Used in manufacture of soap, margarine, brake fluid. Can cause contact dermatitis. (Pharmacy, Natural Food Store, Grocery)

Eucalyptus Oil
Colourless aromatic essential oil from large evergreen native to Australia. Camphor-like odour, pungent cool and spicy. Antiseptic. May cause allergic reactions in sensitive people. Toxic if swallowed. (Natural Food Store, Essential Oil Supplier)

Fuller's Earth
Highly absorbent clay so named from its use in textiles to clean (full) cloth by removing grease. Mined in Florida, England, Canada. Grease-stain remover. Powder for sensitive infants. (Pharmacy)

Glycerine (Glycerol)
Compound of carbon, hydrogen and oxygen, it is a component of all animal and vegetable fats and oils. Clear, colourless, oily, sweet liquid, soluble in water and alcohol, a by-product of fermentation and soapmaking. Used widely in cosmetics, confectionery, explosives. Solvent, humectant, emollient. (Pharmacy)

Lanolin
Purified form of wool grease or wool wax. Translucent, soft, unctuous brown jelly, miscible with water. Used as super-fat in cosmetics, pharmaceuticals. Base, emollient, emulsifier. Can cause allergic reactions. (Pharmacy)

Lard
Semi-solid oil produced by rendering hog's fat. Emollient, base. (Butcher)

Lavender *(Lavandula spp.)*
Aromatic shrub of mint family native to Medi-

terranean, cultivated for flowers and leaves which yield fragrant perfume oil. Possible contact dermatitis, photosensitivity. Absorption through skin can cause stomach upsets, headaches, chills, (Natural Food Store, Essential Oil Supplier)

Mineral Oil
Also known as liquid petrolatum, a by-product of the petroleum refining industry. Colourless transparent oil used extensively in cosmetics. Emollient, binder. (Pharmacy, Grocery)

Neat's-foot Oil
Made by boiling cattle shinbones and feet in water. Pale yellow oil soluble in alcohol. Used mainly as leather softener and preservative. Emollient. Possible allergic reactions. (Hardware)

Ochre
Earth naturally coloured by iron oxides varying from pale yellow to deep red, brown, violet.

Inorganic colorant. (Pharmacy)

Paraffin
Derivative of petroleum industry. Solid, waxy translucent substance in a mixture of hydrocarbons. Soluble in warm alcohol, olive oil. Used in cosmetics as a protective film, base. Rarely can irritate skin. (Grocery, Hardware)

Patchouli *(Pogostemon spp.)*
An East Indian herb of the mint family whose leaves yield a fragrant oil used in soaps and perfumes. Aromatic. Possible allergic reactions. (Natural Food Store, Essential Oil Supplier)

Petroleum Jelly (Petrolatum)
A fatty, translucent jelly-like substance, by-product of petroleum industry. Soluble in oil. Melting point 140 degrees F. Widely used in cosmetics. Emollient. (Grocery, Pharmacy)

Pumice

Spongy, porous volcanic lava used in cleaning, polishing, and scouring compounds. Abrasive. Excessive use can irritate dry or sensitive skin. (Pharmacy, Hardware)

Rosin

Brittle, easily crumbled resin, derived by steam distillation of sap of pine trees. Translucent amber chips soluble in alcohol, oil. Used in varnishes, ointments, by musicians, trapeze artists, baseball pitchers, pool players. Thickener, stiffener. Possible contact dermatitis. (Pharmacy, Music Store)

Saffron

Orange powder from dried stigmas of saffron crocus. Royal colour in early Greece, sprinkled on streets of Rome when Nero entered. Ingredient of early medicines. Used in cooking, dyeing. Natural colorant. (Grocery, Natural Food Store, Gourmet Food Shop)

Sassafras *(Sassafras albidum)*

A North American tree of the laurel family, its bark yields an oil used as flavouring and antiseptic. Aromatic plant parts have been used as tea and aromatic stimulants. Possible allergic rashes. (Essential Oil Supplier)

Strawberry

Fruit and leaves are used as astringent in cosmetics. Essential oil widely used in cosmetics, shampoos and bath products. Possible allergic reactions. (Essential Oil Supplier)

Sulphur

Pale yellow, non-metallic crystalline element widely found in volcanic areas. Used in the manufacture of matches, vulcanized rubber, skin ointments. Insecticide, fungicide, antiseptic, keratolytic. Can irritate skin. Possible allergic reactions. (Pharmacy)

Talc (Magnesium silicate)

Soft, greasy hydrous compound of magnesium

and silica. Used in powders and tooth preparations. Base. (Pottery Supply House, Pharmacy)

Tallow
Hard fat obtained by rendering beef or mutton fat. By extension, any fat, animal or vegetable. Emollient. Possible allergic skin rashes. (Butcher)

Ultramarine
Originally powdered lapis lazuli, worth its weight in gold. Made synthetically from equal amounts of china clay, sulphur, soda ash with some silica and rosin, primary ingredient of laundry blueing. Soluble in oil. (Grocery)

Umber (Hydrated ferric oxide)
Occurring naturally as a mineral earth, in its natural state known as raw umber, and when heated, burnt umber. Inorganic colorant. (Pottery Supply House)

Vanilla
A tall climbing orchid with fragrant flowers and bean from which oil is extracted. Used extensively in cooking and cosmetics. (Grocery, Essential Oil Supplier)

Vitamin E Oil
see Anti-oxidant, page 116 (Natural Food Store)

Wheat Germ Oil
see Anti-oxidant, page 116 (Natural Food Store)

10
A Soaper's Vocabulary

"Skill to do comes of doing."

— *Emerson*

Abrasives are gritty powders that rub or wear away: often used as polishing agents.

Absorbents add bulk by attracting moisture.

Adsorbents condense and hold a protective film to the skin.

Alkalis neutralize acid, soften skin, serve as soap base.

Allergens, even in minute amounts, cause a reaction (rash, asthma, etc.) in persons sensitized to the substance.

Anaesthetics desensitize the body, thereby relieving pain, itching; topical anaesthetics react on body surface only, causing "cool" sensation.

Anti-irritants reduce inflammation.

Anti-oxidants retard deterioration by preventing ingredients such as free fat from combining with oxygen.

Antiseptics prevent spoilage by inhibiting the growth of bacteria in the product and on the skin.

Aromatics have an agreeable fragrance; many are also antiseptic.

Astringents tend to contract skin tissues, making them appear temporarily smoother.

Attar is a sweet flower extract; also known as otto.

Bases form the major part of a cosmetic product, i.e., talc is the base of dusting powder.

Binders provide cohesion among other ingredients to prevent separating.

Blueing makes fabrics look whiter by absorbing blue dye which counteracts yellowness; less light is reflected so it does not make clothes "brighter."

Builders increase the efficiency of a surfactant by counteracting water hardness.

Colour (natural) derives from plants or animals.

Colour (inorganic) derives from minerals or their chemical duplicates.

Colour (synthetic) derives from petrochemical laboratory products (formerly coal tar derivatives) which have never existed in nature.

Demulcents relieve and restore mucous membranes (see anti-irritant).

Detergents clean surfaces by means of emulsifying dirt; either soapy or soapless (synthetic).

Disinfectants purify contamination.

Emollients soften and soothe the skin, i.e. oils and waxes.

Emulsifiers facilitate mixing of ordinarily unmixable liquids such as oil and water.

Essence is a solution of a volatile plant oil in alcohol; also known as "spirit."

Extract is the substance which is drawn out of a plant by means such as distillation, i.e. citronella oil is an extract of tropical grasses.

Fillers add bulk or extend a product.

Fixatives stabilize perfumes so fragrance doesn't evaporate.

Humectants prevent drying by absorbing moisture from the air.

Irritants cause reaction (i.e. rash) in all people exposed to it; reaction decreases with smaller proportion.

Keratolytics loosen superficial dead skin cells so they flake off.

Optical brighteners make fabrics look whiter and brighter by absorbing dyestuffs which increase the proportion of light reflected, particularly on the blue side of the spectrum.

pH indicates the balance of acid and alkali in a product, neutral being 7.

Photosensitizers cause the skin to react (i.e. rash) when exposed to the sun's rays.

Preservatives retard the growth of bacteria or fungi, in a product, making it more resistant to decay.

Protective films coat the skin with a thin layer of proteins, oils or waxes, making it smooth and guarding against moisture, heat, dirt.

Saponins yield soap-like suds when wetted; resistant to chemical analysis.

Soap is a cleanser formed by the union of a fatty acid with a base.

Solvents dissolve other substances, i.e. water, alcohol, acetone.

Stabilizers keep emulsions well-mixed.

Surfactants reduce the surface tension of liquid molecules, allowing them to spread, evenly wetting the surface.

Tincture is extracted by steeping the substance in a solvent, usually alcohol.

11 Sources

"Wash me and I will be whiter than snow."

— *Psalms 51:7*

Essential Oils

The more common oils such as eucalyptus, citronella and cloves can usually be obtained through local pharmacies, craft shops or natural food stores. The smaller quantities will naturally be much more expensive than buying in bulk, but bear in mind that very little is used in each recipe. You might try convincing your local natural foods outlet or craft shop to purchase the oils in bulk for redistribution at a lower price.

WIDE WORLD OF HERBS
9 Ste. Catherine St. E.
Montreal, Quebec
H2X 1K3
Stocks wide variety of natural essential oils in small quantities, although expensive.

BUSH BOAKE ALLEN CORPORATION LTD.
312 St. Patrick
Lasalle, Quebec
H8N 2H2
Minimum 2 kg. containers and minimum invoice $100. Best

price. Will quote to order.

SEELEY & CO. (CANADA) LTD.
3 Jody Avenue, Suite A
Downsview, Ontario
M3N 1H3
Minimum 2 kg. containers. Wide range of oils and compounded fragrances. Will quote to order. No minimum invoice.

LEWISCRAFT
40 Commander Blvd.
Scarborough, Ontario
M1S 3S2
Some synthetic fragrances but no natural ones. Catalogue on request.

Fine Vegetable Oils

Many of the oils such as safflower, peanut, rapeseed, olive and coconut can be purchased at your grocery or natural foods store. Although coconut and olive oils are also available at drugstores, they are packaged in such small quantities that the price is inflated. Delicatessens often yield the best coconut oil price.

Coconut oil can be purchased in large quantities (20 kg. tins) from Canada Packers. Although they will not sell to individuals, it can be ordered through a local bakery, meat packer or retail outlet that already has an account. Palm oil, castor oil and many others are also available from this source.

Moulding Materials

Most hobby shops or craft supply stores will have some materials for making rigid and flexible moulds. They will also carry a variety of plastic candle moulds that can be adapted for soapmaking. The following are mail-order sources for moulds and moulding materials. Catalogues on request, $1.00.

LEWISCRAFT
40 Commander Blvd.
Scarborough, Ontario
M1S 3S2
Moulding materials such as plaster, poly-art, Rubbertex, Insta-mold. Rigid polyethylene, flexible 3D moulds.

Colorants

Synthetic candle dyes can be obtained from the craft supply houses mentioned above or from your local hobby shop. Inorganic colours (mineral earths) can be had from the pottery supply houses listed below or in small quantities from a local potter.

STRATFORD CLAY SUPPLY
P.O. Box 344
Stratford, Ontario
N5A 6T3
Catalogue on request. Excellent service.

TUCKER'S POTTERY SUPPLIES
15 W. Pearce St.
Richmond Hill, Ontario
L4B 1H6

THE POTTERY SUPPLY HOUSE
P.O. Box 192
Oakville, Ontario
L6J 5A2
Catalogue on request.

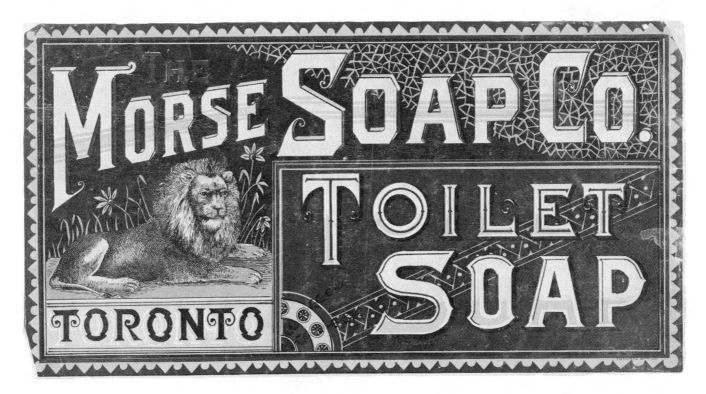

12

Bibliography

"Above all things, keep clean. It is not necessary to be a pig in order to raise one."

— *Ingersoll*

Technical References

Brannt, W.T., *Manufacture of Soaps and Candles.* Philadelphia, 1888.

Canadian Consumer, Volume 8, No. 1, July/August 1970. "Soap: It's been around for 2,000 years" p. 9, 29.

Canadian Consumer, Volume 7, No. 3, June 1977. "Test: Soaps" p. 12

Carmichael, John, *A Treatise on Soapmaking.* New York: Collins & Perkins, 1810.

Coon, Nelson, *The Dictionary of Useful Plants.* Pennsylvania: Rodale Press, Book Division, 1974.

Cristiani, R.S., *A Technical Treatise on Soap & Candles.* Philadelphia: Henry Carey Baird & Co., 1881.

Deite, Carl, *Manual of Toilet Soapmaking.* New York: D. Van Nostrand Company, n.d.

Hobson, Phyllis, *Making Homemade Soaps & Candles.* Vermont: Garden Way Publishing, 1975.

Hurst, Geroge H., *Soaps: A Practical Manual of the*

Manufacture of Domestic, Toilet and other Soaps. London: Scott, Greenwood, & Co., 1898.

Hylton, Wm. H., ed., *The Rodale Herb Book.* Pennsylvania: Rodale Press, 1974.

Krochmal, Connie, *A Guide to Natural Cosmetics.* New York: Quadrangle, 1973.

Moore, Elaine, *Detergents.* A Unilever Educational Booklet, 1973.

Morfit, Campbell, *A Practical Treatise on the Manufacture of Soaps.* New York: John Wiley & Son, 1871.

Plummer, Beverley, *Fragrance: How to Make Natural Soaps, Scents, and Sundries.* New York: Atheneum, 1975.

Poucher, W.A., *Perfumes, Cosmetics & Soaps.* London: Chapman & Hall, 1974.

Richter, Dorothy, *Make Your Own Soaps, Plain and Fancy.* New York: Doubleday & Co. Inc., 1974.

Sagarin, Edward, *The Science and Art of Perfumery.* New York: Greenberg, 1955.

Stark, Norman, *The Formula Book.* Kansas City: Sheed and Ward, Inc., 1975.

Verrill, A. Hyatt, *Perfumes and Spices.* Boston: L.C. Page & Co., 1940.

Wigner, J.H., *Soap Manufacture.* New York: Chemical Publishing Co. Inc., 1940.

Historical References

A "Canuck," *Early Pioneer Life in Upper Canada.* Toronto: William Briggs, 1905.

Conant, Thomas, *Upper Canada Sketches.* Toronto: William Briggs, 1898.

Douville, Raymond, *La vie quotidienne des Indiens du Canada a l'epoque de la colonisation francaise.* Paris: Hachette, 1967.

Guillet, Edwin C., *Pioneer Arts & Crafts.* Toronto: University of Toronto Press, 1940.

Hopwood, Victor G., ed., *David Thompson: Travels*

126   *in Western North America 1784-1812.* Toronto: Macmillan, 1971.

MacIntyre, D.E., *Prairie Storekeeper.* Toronto: Peter Martin.

McLean, John, *Canadian Savage Folk: The Native Tribes of Canada.* Toronto: William Briggs, 1896.

Reader, W.J., *Unilever: A Short History.* London: Unilever House, 1960.

Robertson, Heather, *Salt of the Earth.* Toronto: James Lorimer & Company, 1974.

Sigerist, Henry E., *Civilization & Disease.* University of Chicago Press: Phoenix Books, 1962.

Stephenson, H.E. and NcNaught, Carlton, *The Story of Advertising in Canada.* Toronto: The Ryerson Press, 1940.

Styles, W.A.L., *Unusual Facts of Canadian History.* Toronto: McClelland & Stewart Ltd., 1947.

Thwaites, Reuben Gold, Ed., *The Jesuit Relations and Allied Documents. Volume XXXVIII.* Cleveland: 1899.

Tivy, Louis, *Your Loving Anna: Letters from the Ontario Frontier.* Toronto: University of Toronto Press, 1972.

Twain, Mark, "The Facts Concerning the Recent Resignation," from *The Oxford Dictionary of Quotations.* Toronto: Oxford University Press, 1941

Vogel, Virgil J., *American Indian Medicine.* Norman: University of Oklahoma Press, 1970.

Warrington, C.J.S. and Nicholls, R.V.V., *A History of Chemistry in Canada.* Toronto: Sir Isaac Pitman and Sons, 1949.

Wood, William, *New England's Prospect.* Boston: Thomas and John Fleet, 1764.

Wright, Lawrence, *Clean & Decent.* London: Routledge & Kegan Paul, 1960.

Other References

Andrews, Wm. A. Ed., *A Guide to the Study of Environmental Pollution.* Scarborough: Prentice-Hall, 1972.

Fisher, John, *What You Can Do About Pollution Now.* Toronto: Longman Canada Ltd., 1971.

Rapaport, Howard, M.D. and Motter, Shirly, M.S., *The Complete Allergy Guide.* New York: Simon and Schuster, 1970.

Rinzler, Carol Ann, *Cosmetics: What the Ads Don't Tell You.* Toronto: Fitzhenry & Whiteside Ltd., 1977.

Sheffe, Norman, Ed., *Issues for the Seventies: Environmental Quality.* Toronto: McGraw-Hill Company of Canada, 1971.

Swinny, Boen, M.D., *Conquering Your Allergy.* New York: Fleet Publishing Corporation, 1959.

Taub, Harold, *Keeping Healthy in a Polluted World.* New York: Harper & Row, 1974.

Vallentyne, John R., *The Algal Bowl.* Ottawa: Department of the Environment, Fisheries & Marine Service, 1974.

Statistical Information

The following organizations have provided indispensible statistical information:

Pollution Probe
University of Toronto
Toronto, Ontario
M5S 1A1

Fisheries & Environment Canada
Detergent Control Unit
Water Pollution Control Directorate
Environmental Protection Service
Ottawa, Ontario
K1A 1C8

Statistics Canada
Central Inquiries
User Advisory Services Division
Ottawa, Ontario
K1A 0T6